to Kiaya Jael, Kaleah Jade, & Jude King

IN THE TRENCHES: 10 Reasons to Stay in Ministry

Published by Waterspings Media House, LLC.
P.O. Box 1284
Olive Branch, MS 38654
Contact publisher for permission requests and bulk orders.
www.waterspringsmedia.com

Printed in the United States of America.

Library of Congress Control Number: 2018934154

ISBN 13: 978-0-9988249-8-7
ISBN 10: 0-9988249-8-4

Jenean,
May God bless you
as you follow Him into the
trenches. Thanks
Josh Nelson

Into the Trenches

10 Reasons to Stay in Ministry

BY JOSHUA C. NELSON

Contents

■■■

Foreword

Few who have engaged in gospel ministry for some time will deny that ministry is no cake walk. To be a leader of God's people in the closing scenes of earth's history is an undertaking that calls for dedication and tenacity, not to mention creativity and connectivity to God. More significantly, doing ministry today seems to be inherently lonely and trying, with the result that many ministers, on at least one occasion, have seriously considered quitting ministry and going back to fishing.

In this book, Joshua Nelson reflects on his ministerial journey with insight and incisiveness. Transparent almost to a fault, the author bares his soul, revealing his struggles, insecurities, and shortcomings. Nelson is not afraid to admit that he has questioned his call and flirted with turning in his credentials. Like so many others, for a while ministry had become meaningless for him, an unbalanced dance of muddled priorities that left him feeling unfulfilled and empty. Yet Nelson is not content to reveal the underside of ministry, leaving his readers depressed and clueless. With admirable skill, he shares 10 compelling reasons pastors should persist in ministry. The first is that God has called you, God's worker, and the last is that victory is gained or experienced in the trenches, the metaphor the author uses to capture and convey the essence of ministry. Each of the reasons is unpacked rather neatly and deftly by Nelson.

Conflict is almost synonymous with church nowadays, and a conflict-free ministry may very well indicate that the enemy's kingdom is not being upset or upended in any way, the fourth point Nelson underscores. That ministry may be summed up or characterized as an intense conflict raging in the trenches is very much on target, and one does not have to engage in ministry for an extended period of time to arrive at that conclusion. Members seem to experience a certain measure of glee in creating havoc and provoking ill will in our churches, with not a few acting as though their calling or giftedness is keeping their pastor on his or her knees.

This valuable book should resonate with every minister or lay leader and will rescue and encourage them simultaneously. The author's style is winsome and engaging, and Nelson uses personal experiences to illustrate and unpack his ideas which are profound and sure to trigger introspection and reflection. Readers should prepare to be informed and inspired as they listen to the author's story, which, I am sure, will intersect with theirs on multiple levels.

The privilege and joy were mine to have Joshua Nelson in class at the Seventh-day Adventist Theological Seminary at Andrews University. He performed with distinction, earning the highest grade possible. I found Pastor Nelson to be wise beyond his years, and a serious student with a deep appreciation for scholarship. I have no qualms in recommending *Into the Trenches:*

10 Reasons to Stay in Ministry, firmly believing that a pastor or lay leader who is thinking of quitting ministry will, at the very least, reconsider after reading this book.

R. Clifford Jones, President
Lake Region Conference,
Seventh Day Adventist Church

Prologue

It was hot and muggy, the air conditioning struggled to keep the car and its occupant cool. The sweat still dribbled from my brow and slowly soaked the collar of my shirt. I still had about two more hours to drive before reaching the midsize North Carolina city, whose prideful trait, was a fort called Bragg. The car rumbled over some loose gravel on the asphalt, almost jostling me out of my dull thoughts about the upcoming events. This was going to be an interesting new life and I wondered how I would manage everything. How would the church like me? Would they accept me? Would I be able to handle the task ahead of me? What about all the horror and war stories my predecessors had told me? Would I last? Would the employment office approve of me? But what really shook me to the core was the secret question us full-time ministers ask, despite all the proof, signs, and visions, "Am I truly called to the ministry?" But there was no time for that kind of questioning now, this would be my first church district. I would be placed in a new setting on a new journey. I'd better man up and not show any weakness. I was only 22 years old and fresh from college, an HBCU in the south, but still preaching like a west coast boy from California. I had spent my four college years in Alabama, but that was for school and for some reason the Carolinas just felt different. The air was thicker, the gnats seemed angrier, and the sun felt hotter. I noticed some immediate differences in the geography. There were no mountains that could be seen anywhere. Swamps seemed to be everywhere. Abandoned houses littered the countryside like broken time machines straining to hold on to a distant past. And the most notable sight for me was the deep, grassy, muddy trenches lining the roads. It would be terrible if I veered off into one of them, but more motivation to stay awake, I thought, as I continued to drive.

I began to panic just a little but quickly forced the feeling from thickening the lump in my throat. And then the questions began again. How would I ever survive in the south amongst southern preachers steeped in a rich church tradition? As this thought twirled through my mind, suddenly red lights flashed in front of me waking me from the tumult of questions swirling around in my head. The car stopped, and the lights were solid red now, we wouldn't be going anywhere fast anytime soon. This was something I did not expect; country traffic. You could almost feel the wind gushing from the vehicles speeding past on the opposite side of the median as if to taunt the stagnant situation of those northbound on Highway 95. You could almost see the faces of the people zipping past shaking their heads as if to say, "You all will be sitting there for a long time." I sighed and mentally settled in for a long game of ankle pumping. As my car inched closer to the source of our delay, I could see and hear the flashing lights and sirens.

If I didn't know any better, I would say the entire police, fire, and emergency department of North Carolina was out on the freeway. It seemed like an eternity until I finally saw it. A car stood at an angle of 45 degrees in the nearby trench. I felt bad for those people as they looked on at their trenched vehicle, they were blessed to be alive. I felt peace for them because at least they had help as firemen and EMS workers scrambled to help. The good nature of people seems to come out the most during a crisis. For some reason we are more willing to help someone we do not know with an immediate problem then to assist people we do know with long term problems.

As the police waved me by, the huge crane lifted the car out of the deep ditch with a loud suck then "pop" the car was free. I knew my slowing down to watch would just create more traffic, but I couldn't help but become fixated on the trench. I rubbed my eyes, thinking maybe my contact lenses were playing tricks on me. There was a man still stuck in the trench where the car had been. His hand waved as one hand gripped the side of the trench as he tried to crawl out. No one seemed to notice. I tried to push down my power windows and shout, but no one heard me. The cars behind me began to honk as I slowed, squinted, blinked, fighting to see the man stuck in the trench. Something wasn't right. Just before the waving hand was out of sight, the man pulled his body up just enough for me to see his face. I cranked my neck back one last time, stabilizing the car with my hand and knee, then I saw him. He crawled out of the trench wearing a full suit soiled from the mud, grass throughout his hair, and in his hand a black worn Bible.

I never really understood this image of the suited man in the trench until recently. In many ways this story has become an allegory for my ministry. Little did I know on that hot Carolina day, that I was not only heading to my first pastoral assignment, I was diving head on into a muddy, grassy trench called ministry.

Chapter 1: The Rare Beast

Strangely, He has called us into the trenches.

Lamentations 3:53-55, CEB
"They caught me alive in a pit and threw stones at me; water flowed over my head. I thought: I'm finished. I call on your name, Lord, from the depths of the pit."

■■■

I know, you're wondering who begins a book quoting the saddest book in the Bible. But this is where we must begin. We start in the pit or as I like to say, the trench. When I was a boy my grandfather told me his war stories from his experiences in the second world war. I remember reading stories about WWII and the differences between it and WWI. One huge difference was the use of trench warfare, which was quite deadly, during WWI. The idea was that you could dig a large trench where your men could hide opposite the enemies trench. At the most strategic moment you would rush out of the pit and storm the enemies side. This served to be a literal death trap as the machine gun became more prevalent in the war. Men in the trench could hear the rapid fire of bullets whizzing over their heads as officers screamed for them to attack. They rose above the pit, mostly to sudden death, as the bullets riddled their bodies. Many falling back into the very pits they had just climbed out of. In the remake of the movie "Wonder Woman," there is an amazing scene when she climbs out of the trench and shields the gunfire with her shield subsequently taking back the field. This is how I think I look when preaching a powerful sermon, leading a community project, or finishing a successful small group. But the reality is that most times that evening or later the next week I fall right back into the trench I fought so valiantly to get out of.

A life dedicated to ministry is not far different then a life pledged to serving your country. In some countries doing ministry actually renders literal risk on your life. In some places this risk is even more dangerous for a minister than a solider. Growing up I was fascinated by stories of missionaries deep in the jungles and forests of unknown regions of our world. They were the ones really on the front lines of this thing called ministry. Anything I planned to do in America would pale in comparison to the literal life and death struggles they faced. But still I wake up in the morning feeling emotionally and spiritually drained. I feel like I am there in the trenches of Africa, the Amazon, Russia, or WWI, trapped in a situation where I do not know how to win. And although I am smart enough to know that my situation pales in comparison to missionaries oversees, I cannot help but feel like giving up.

Maybe you too have felt like quitting on ministry. There have been times when, like me, you woke up saying this would be your last day. And let me be clear, this trench ministry is not reserved just for pastors. Anyone involved in ministry, whether bible work, holding a church position, working a non-profit, or any area of active Christian service, knows the trench feeling. A trench can be a low in your life, a difficult spell in your ministry, a personal spiritual battle, or a family tragedy. My trenches have come in a variety of ways. Threats on my life, the loss of our daughter, harsh criticism, verbal abuse, and fights in the church have been some of my largest trenches.

A trench can seem daunting to climb out of, but it is possible. If we have someone to remind us why we are on the battle field, we can begin to find reason for the trench. We must go back to answer the question of why we answered the call in the first place.

I answered this call to ministry like most Christians because that is what Jesus had asked me to do. He gave us the Great Commission. He called us to a higher status as we recognized the "priesthood of all believers". He woke me up in the middle of the night and placed a burden on my heart for souls. A burden I later learned was the call to full-time ministry for God. I had answered the call. I had done the work. I studied, prayed, got my degrees, received my job, and bowed low as the Elders ordained me. I did all of this for Jesus, but now where was He in my darkest moments? Was this all a rouse? A charade? I thought pastoral ministry was going to be about preaching powerful messages and watching as the word spread that there was a young dynamic preacher in town. I thought thousands would come. They would come with their sick and their lame, their tired and their poor, they would come from near and far to just see a man who preached about the Man. They would come and they would leave changed. They would be baptized and they would be on fire. I would have my diamond studded crown waiting for me in glory and all would be right with my ministry. I am struggling not to insert multiple laughing tear emojis. Instead of this I was faced with maybe thirty people on a good day coming to hear my sermons. Senior members who had already put their work in years before and weren't ready to jump back in the trench, simply because a boy told them they must. Then there were the working-class members who never had time and commitment to do real evangelism or lacked passionate spirituality. And of course, the youth who were not reliable and never seemed enthused about anything. Not to mention the multiple issues, problems, differences of opinions, arguments, distractions, complaints, and sometimes straight rebellion demonstrated by the people of God.

Aside from church issues, ministry just wasn't very fruitful. The community had heard the gospel preached and had settled into their own clichés and denominations. Unchurched people were used to dismissing you or using you, whichever was most beneficial. Any visions or innovative ministry ideas were either being done on the government level or apathy hindered us from trying. I got angry. I was upset. Why couldn't I just do ministry? Then I realized this was ministry, or at least a part of it.

The Smell of Ministry

Sidestepping I barely missed the uneven concrete slab only to stumble on some loose rocks. This obstruction married well with the many cracks that littered the Chicago sidewalk. The gutter broke my fall but now splashes of a mysterious mixture of possibly mud, oil, and please don't tell me, sunk into my sneakers. My girlfriend, helped me back onto the sidewalk as we continued walking through the neighborhood. Armed with bags of lunches, long stares joined our shadows in pursuit as we trudged towards the park. As we turned the corner, a group of unsavory characters crowded the path. They let us pass as a thick cloud of smoke engulfed us. We stifled a few coughs and continued on our way. The smell of smoke lingered in our nostrils laced with the hard smell of liquor. At the crosswalk we could see the park ahead of us where many homeless gathered. As we waited for the light to turn, a bit of tangled weave blew across the street. The woman on my arm started to sigh, I could feel she was ready to get back on the bus and head back to the church. I turned to her and smiled, then said, "Take it all in, take a deep breath, do you smell that?"

She hesitated and then looked at me bewildered and said, "yes, why?"

The light changed colors and we began to cross the street. "That's the smell of ministry", I declared.

There are times when you can just smell ministry opportunities. Whenever you are uncomfortable or out of your normal routine these are times when Christians are alerted to ministry. We welcome these experiences because we welcome the hardship of others and all the sounds, smells, looks, and stares that come with it. We are the ones called out to go into the valley and find the least, the last, and the lost. We desire to guide them out of the shadows and into the light, so the glory of the Son may shine upon them. We love the smell of ministry because it tells us we are in a place where Jesus would be. We are following Him into the corners forgotten, filled with power and hope. The work is hard, but we keep going back because we are addicted to the chase. We are obsessed with seeing the Holy Spirit catch hold of the drug addict, the orphan, the single mother, the depressed, the molested, the downtrodden, even the rich, the wealthy but poor in spirit.

We stay in the trench because we desperately want just one more, just one more soul to be saved. We ignore the discomfort; we ignore the pain for as long as we can, sometimes loving this more than dealing with those agitators in our own church. But after a while burnout still sets in and we get weak. We look up and notice the ministry trench and we want to get out.

What is the Trench?

Now you may not be in full-time ministry, you may just be reading for encouragement in a low time in your Christian walk: or as a lay leader or someone involved in community advancement. But whatever your area of ministry we must understand that the trench can catch any of us. And what we first learn is that ministry is not a goal or an accomplishment, ministry is the people. We want to bypass the bureaucracy to do what we think is ministry, but that is ministry.

It's hard to define ministry because ministry is alive, it breathes, it changes. There are no "one-size-fits-all" descriptions of what ministry must be defined as. However, I think that there are some stories in the bible and some principles that point us to experiences that say, "Yes, that is ministry." And I believe that in every last ministry example the focal word is "selflessness."

Ministry is about being attentive to the needs of others. This is why ministry is more than preaching a "good message." Ministry is about the needs and concerns of others. As we will see later, ministry involves jumping in someone else's trench. Because of this, ministry is often extremely taxing and difficult. It will not always fit into your fun category or comfort scale. It will bring about stress, strain, and fear. It will require resolve, dedication, consistency, and an overactive prayer life. Ministry takes a toll on your life in numerous ways. It will affect your choice in a spouse, or your current marriage, your family life, where you live and the quality of life, your income and career dreams, what jobs you take or do not take, your health, the way you see life, etc.

If you are not careful, you will burn yourself out which is why I believe ministry is also about how well you minister to yourself. Remember, even David said he had to encourage himself (1 Sam 30:6). It is important to remember that taking care of you is not selfish because you are doing self-preservation so you can do ministry more effectively. This is often a mistake many have made and still make. They allow ministry to literally stress them out to the point of death. They fall into the trenches and stay there unable or unwilling to climb out and fight. God asks us to die spiritually and in some cases, die physically, but that death should not be at your own irresponsible hand. This is the part of trench ministry that is dangerous to your life and to the calling.

The trench is that place of hardship or as David calls it, *"the valley of the shadow of death"* (Psalm 23:4). It is a place in your Christian life that leaves you questioning your purpose and searching for relevance. It is the place God often takes us. It is the place where we often find Him.

Tackle the Beast

When I was younger I had this odd definition for ministry. I called ministry "that rare beast that everyone has been called to tackle." What I meant was that ministry is strange and different, but also large and difficult to handle. It is something you have never faced before, a new challenge, a new adventure, and/or a new trench. But even though it is hairy and crude, God has called all, not just Pastors, to tackle this animal called ministry. It becomes your life purpose to do ministry any way God calls you to do it. Whatever your career or occupation you have an obligation to tackle that beast. If you are an extravert or introvert, loud or quiet, a Bible scholar or new believer, the task is still at hand. You still are asked to minister to someone who is in need of Jesus.

Our Christian ministry assignment is revealed in countless ways. That is why it should not be defined by or confined to a few roles. I believe God has called everyone to a personal ministry because God is asking everyone to tell somebody about Him. You can engage in this on a small scale or a large one, however, trench ministry is going to take you to a place of discomfort. As humans, we do not like to be uncomfortable, we do not like to suffer. In looking at the life of Jesus I found that true ministry is not always comfortable. In fact, in some cases you will know you are doing ministry when it becomes uncomfortable.

Paul often spoke of trials, sufferings, and thorns that ministry brought on. Jesus famously said in John 15:18, *"If the world hates you, keep in mind it hated me first."* And so, ministry is the extension of the great controversy that we engage this fight between good and evil. When you do this, you are placing yourself as a warrior amidst an age-old war between God and Satan. It will not always bring about the results you think you should see either. Because ministry, like in many wars, it is hard to measure success. It's really more of an inward gage between you and God to know if you are really giving of yourself. It is God who ultimately provides the increase. Our job is to simply be faithful and show people Jesus.

One of my favorite preachers, Henry Wright in his 2011 sermon *"The Doctrine of Ministry"* preached at the Pastoral Evangelism Leadership Council held at Oakwood University Church, he reminded us that Jesus walked this earth and only won 12, and He was God on earth. And even those twelve abandoned Him when He needed them most. We cannot be distracted by how we wish to gage our effectiveness in ministry. The key is to remember that ministry begins when you are on your knees. Christ's example shows us that He would get up early in the morning and spend time with God. If this is not a current practice of any full-time ministers or lay ministers, you will probably have trouble remaining in ministry.

The first lesson that I learned that helped give me a reason not to quit was knowing that ministry is not always easy. Jesus said that in the world we would have tribulation. Paul spoke about glorying in his sufferings. Prophets were killed. Disciples murdered. Christians burned. Jesus crucified. Why did I think ministry would be any different for me? In fact, if ministry was easy then I would probably have to question if what I was doing could even be classified as ministry.

I remember that John the Baptist was left in the prison to die, even while Jesus was walking the earth. Read that again! John died in his trench while Jesus walked by. One of my favorite authors, Dietrich Bonhoeffer famously said in his book *Cost of Discipleship*, "When Christ calls a Man, He bids him come and die." These examples and this quote have been some of my themes throughout my short time in full-time ministry. It reminds me that I have been called to be a witness or as the Greek would word it, a Martyr. I have been called by God to go, not to sit and wait around, but to march forward into a world that will hate me. So, start your march toward the cliff, the fire, the pain. Jesus tells us to preach an unpopular message to a populated world who needs to denounce its sin and acknowledge its Savior. His commission is for me to be a Martyr to HIM and for HIM. And for some reason, we loved Him enough and desired to follow Him everywhere, even to the cross. We picked up our cross and followed Him, and now we cannot forget that the cross leads us to Calvary. To a place of pain but also a place of victory. You are in the pain right now. You are struggling to carry the cross right now. But know that this is normal. Ministry is war.

A Prophet in the Pit

Jeremiah was a prophet that knew about pain all too well. He was told to preach an unpopular message to his people. I can only imagine the strength and boldness you need to preach rebukes for your entire ministry. Not a message of victory, hope, or love, but a message of failure and captivity. Jeremiah went as far to say they might as well give up and turn themselves in to the besieging Babylonian army. As would be expected, the officials told the king to put Jeremiah to death. The Bible says that King Zedekiah gives the officers permission to take hold of Jeremiah. These officers weren't playing any games or taking any chances with Jeremiah and his discouraging sermons. They put him in a pit so deep they had to lower him down with ropes. The text makes a point to mention that there was no water in the pit (or cistern) except for the water that mixed with the dirt (Jeremiah 38:6). So not only is Jeremiah in a deep dark hole with no water, not only was he alone, but he was also sinking into the mud. This is probably the premier example of a ministry trench. Alone. Ineffective. Stuck. Uncomfortable. Misunderstood.

#TrenchChronicles

One of the most difficult aspects of pastoral ministry is being misunderstood. As mentioned before, I started full-time ministry at age 22 where most people I pastored were two or three times my age. In my first district there was an elder who was 100 years old. Being young in ministry has its difficulties and especially for me since I look five years younger than I am. I will never forget that first worship service in my very first church.

Graduation had been in May and it was now July. I had spent June with my cousins in Las Vegas (hey, we had to visit my grandparents so don't judge me). To say the least, I was wet behind the ears. I had no idea what I was getting myself into. The past few months had been so amazing, so fun, but now I entered a building where everyone looked...well they did not look excited, I will put it like that. My parents were in attendance; they had flown in from California. My sister and girlfriend at the time were present. And of course, the conference official was there to introduce me and anoint me before the church.

The church was not very large but for its size it seemed packed. As it usually happens on opening days there were people there the first day that I never saw again. In a small town and small church, I guess word of a young new preacher from California was something to come and see. As I anticipated my entrance into the sanctuary, my parents had been seated first. I overheard someone say upon looking at my father, "Oh wow we sure are getting a young Pastor." I clinched up and began to sweat. If they considered my dad young what would they consider me? Furthermore the tone she used when saying the word "young" just did not sound very endearing. Then it happened. I heard that dreaded four letter word as the sister finally realized I was the pastor she said, "Oh wait, you're the pastor? We have a BABY for a pastor y'all." I still remember anger mixed with fear that I felt as

I walked to the pulpit to preach my sermon that day.

It wasn't a great sermon, some eyes had closed, but I preached well enough. I got through that day, but then the dust settled, family went home, girlfriend became ex-girlfriend, and the conference official went back to the office. I was all alone it seemed. For as long as I minister, I hope to never forget that feeling. As I lay on my air mattress in my relatively empty apartment staring at the white, popcorn ceiling. I said to myself, "Now what?" I felt helpless, vulnerable, unsure of myself. The word "baby" seemed to be etched in my brain. The feeling seemed to hang over me every time I spoke. I struggled to feel the respect I knew my degree deserved. I wondered if I could really do this?

It is what it is

Throughout my short time in ministry (it has been 10 years while I write this) I have experienced much push back because of my age. Some people do not think I am capable or qualified to lead them or the church. It probably is not how most people feel and I am sure my emotions are going overboard but this is how I have felt. My age often seems a point of surprise, contention, or liability rather than a blessing. It seems that people would rather an older man lead and a young man preach. Instead of feeling like people are proud of my decision to follow Christ at a young age, I feel like people are tolerating it.

I think people forget what their words really can do to someone early in their career. A compliment goes a long way, because for me, it isn't about getting puffed up, it's more about confirmation that God is using me and that you were blessed. But instead I have heard many people say they will not compliment the minister because they are keeping him humble. But those same people and others have no problem sharing publicly about all of the faults and shortcomings of the same preacher.

When I turned 30 I really embraced that year of ministry because it was the same age Jesus officially began. I had been reflecting on all that Jesus did when He was my age. It is encouraging to see that He faced problems as well. My mind always goes to that time when Jesus spoke about Abraham as someone He knew personally (John 8:58). The elders were so livid they questioned His age saying, *"Thou art not yet fifty years old, and has thou seen Abraham?" (John 8:57).* Maybe 50 is the golden age when you finally get respect. I can imagine my elders laughing at that statement. I know the disrespect never ends, no matter your age. But this story does give me confidence when I am feeling timid because of my age. Jesus responds with confidence and boldness knowing that they would pick up stones to try and kill Him. I must say, I have not offended a church board yet to that extent. It is easy to forget that Jesus had feelings too when reading these stories. I can only imagine how He must have felt at this point. I cannot imagine it was a good feeling. Sadly, for me when I feel hated or my character is misrepresented, I feel like quitting. At times the desire to leave ministry and move back to California and work at expanding my dad's computer business is quite tempting. It is in these tough moments, the moments when you have to address the ugly side of human character that you must remember who called you and who is leading you.

Reason #1 not to quit ministry:

Your calling was never meant to be easy.

Chapter 2: Cries from the Trench

Cries that echoes from the cross.

Psalm 40: 1-3, NASB
"I waited patiently for the Lord;
And He inclined to me and heard my cry.
He brought me up out of the pit of destruction, out of the miry clay, And He set my feet upon a rock making my footsteps firm.
He put a new song in my mouth, a song of praise to our God;
Many will see and fear and will trust in the Lord."

■■■

I love this verse because David is explaining how he made it out of the trench. The only problem I have with his testimony is that "p" word. It is hard to be patient, especially in the trench.

#TrenchChronicles

It had been a long night. The baby must have woken us up ten times that night. I was exhausted but I crawled my way out of bed to begin my busy day. The day began with a quick breakfast that wasn't nearly enough calories for the energy I needed. With toast in one hand and the steering wheel in the other I made my way to my first appointment. After the morning meeting with the school board, I raced to my office for a counseling session, for which I was already late. From there I went to the jail to visit and mentor one of the young men from my church. Leaving there, I hurried to catch the middle school kids before they ended their lunch. I sat with my other mentee and talked a bit before the bell rang. Now, it was time to grab my own lunch with a few of the pastors in town for a planning meeting. As the meeting ended my phone reminded me I had promised to visit one of the shut-ins from the church. On the way to her house I got an angry call from a member who wasn't pleased with the taste of the communion bread from the previous service. I kindly gave her some ways we could solve the issue as I arrived at the shut-ins house. After a prayer, encouragement, and some laughs I headed back to the office to work a little on my sermon. Just as I opened my Bible there was a knock on my office door. Before I could say a word, the door unlocked and opened as one of my leaders entered. Maybe they didn't realize I was in study, but they proceeded to talk to me for the next thirty minutes before I kindly said I needed to study. That was when my phone rang. The mother on the other end was frantic and needed my help as her daughter had just been suspended from school. It was one of the girls from my youth group who had struggled with addiction and suicide, so I went to meet them. We all came back to the church in time for the youth prayer meeting that I led. As the group ended we transitioned into the sanctuary for the adult prayer service. After the service I was swarmed with people wanting to talk. The entire time I smiled and tried to keep interest in the conversations. For a moment I wavered, and someone noticed and asked if I was even paying attention to them. Another made a joke about how I couldn't be tired since I don't have a "real job". I just looked at them in disbelief. I gathered my things, as I made the necessary pleasantries and laughs. I said a few "God bless you's" and got into my car. I quickly turned on the engine ready to leave. Somehow everyone managed to leave the parking lot before me. I realized the church was still unlocked and lights were left on, so I got out of the car and secured the building. After returning to my car I noticed one of the members was still there and came out of another door which he thankfully locked behind him. I almost escaped but he caught me and talked to me for about fifteen minutes before I could find a polite way to end the conversation. I got into my car, said a prayer and drove the thirty miles to arrive home around 10:00 p.m. I sat in the car and almost cried. This had to stop.

What Ministers Will Not Tell You

I doubt anymore that it's possible to be in ministry and not at least once think of quitting. At one point I probably quit ministry every week in my mind. I truly believe like Jeremiah learned, and especially John the Baptist, it just comes with the territory. You will have doubts. You will be tested. I am often lonely, angry, frustrated, depressed, fragile, and even scared. I often feel like I am in the trench because ministry is trench warfare. The reality is that we are in a war. We must place our issues into perspective and remember that we have been called to become soldiers in this war. There are no bystanders, just fighters or prisoners. We must make a choice every day and look ministry in the eyes and decide to fight another day. This fight is difficult and will bring unknown stresses and trials in your personal life and even your family. Most definitely as a Pastor, but even more as non-clergy who are looking to fulfill Christ's commission while working in another vocation.

When the stress of ministry begins to attack the family, then the strain of the call can feel almost unbearable. It is easy to suffer through when you are single and do what needs to be done to get by, but it is a whole different matter when your spouse and/or children are involved. I have yet to experience the strain ministry can have on my child, but I have seen how it effects my wife. I want to thank God for such an amazing woman in my life. It is the hardest thing in the world to see the strain that my calling has put her through. The devil attacking me is one thing but seeing the attacks of the enemy on my wife is a whole different story. At times it can be unbearable but again I thank God for a praying woman that has taken my call on as her call. In a way, she has become the embodiment of God with me in the trenches of ministry.

Partner in the Trench

God often reminds me that I am not alone in this trench. Jesus, being God himself, had trouble changing the hardness of human hearts (i.e. the Pharisees) in the church. Now this is no reason to throw up your hands and stop trying. Jesus never gave up on the disciples or even those who opposed Him. He appealed to them until the bitter end.

However, it means that I can have peace knowing that I wrestle not against flesh and blood. There are just some things that are out of my control and sphere of influence. It is the job of the Holy Spirit to use me to say the right words and act the right way so that the Holy Spirit can work with the hearer to receive it the right way and with the right attitude. Each person has their own decision to make as to how they will react to the Holy Spirit. Again, my only job is to be responsive to Him. But even that sometimes drives me up the wall because I question if I am truly listening to Him. Maybe there was something else I could have said or maybe if I had just read that book or taken that class more seriously. Maybe it is because I didn't pray enough or spend enough time with certain members. Maybe there was more I could do. And sure, there probably is more that I could do, more that you could do. After what John says at the end of his gospel, maybe Jesus is the only one that couldn't have done more. But even then, you could argue that maybe one more parable would have saved Judas, or just one more sermon on the mount would have reeled in that lost soul. We could question and have this 'what if game' all day. The reality is that people still have a choice as to how they will respond to God's grace.

As ministers we cannot save people. We can try to position people or prepare people, but it is the Spirit's job to convict and move the heart. Re-read Jesus' prayer in John 17 again and ask yourself if Jesus wasn't sharing some of the same emotions we have felt. He prayed for those He ministered to. He knew that they were still struggling with sin. He wanted to make sure He had done all He could and that the father would give power to do the rest. It is interesting that the main thing Jesus wanted from us was oneness, unity. That was the one thing they did not have, even at the end of Jesus' ministry. And that is the one thing that the church and ministry organizations struggle to maintain.

When we are feeling discouraged take a look at Christ and put yourself in His shoes. Read John 19 and reflect on the agony he went through in the garden. Think about how stressed you have to be to sweat drops of blood, then see your closest friends asleep in your moment of need. And this dereliction of duty didn't happen once but three times. And to make matters worse, they all left him when he was arrested. To add salt to the wound, one of his closest friends and future leader of the church denies Him three times. Jesus had to have some kind of faith in His mission, to keep on going through the trench, and up that hill called Calvary.

The problem for me has been my perspective of ministry. I would much rather follow Jesus down the road on a colt then up the road beneath a cross. Ministry feels great when they are screaming your name, giving you high-fives, and calling you blessed. But, the going gets tough when you speak just a little too much truth. When you begin to call out the right sins and speak the right truth to power, that is when your resolve will be tested in ministry. Will you keep on climbing up the hill with Jesus or have you had enough? For many of us we find ourselves in situations where you cannot see past the cross, past the problems that you are facing. Jesus had not been to the cross but He kept marching forward, envisioning victory past the trial.

We have a luxury that He did not have, and this luxury comes because of what He did on that cross. We have hope that is grounded by the resurrection of our Lord. He conquered the trials and because He did we do as well. He was a conqueror and now He makes us more than conquerors. So now we see that there is greater in us and we can overcome the world simply because He already did!

Jesus said, *"In the world you will have tribulation but be of good cheer I have overcome the world (John 16:33)."* When I know that God and I are close, and I can feel him leading me when problems arise I should expect them. In fact, if you are not facing trials as a minister you may want to question who it is you are following. Jesus will send you into the storm, into the fire, into the trench because that is where the fight is. *That is where the conjuring can occur* because He will never send you alone. Our cries in the trench echo from his cries on the cross. The cross is victory. The trench is where victory can take place. You are the one He trusts for ministry. He is placing you in to take the last shot. You are His prodigy, His legacy, His inspiration. We suffer in the trench but thank God for His presence, thank God, the trench has room for two.

▪ Something to Try ▪

Write down the reasons you started active ministry. Reflect on the reasons God has you currently doing ministry. Connect your experience with Christ and find Him in your situation.

Christian Ministry - Any selfless act of service you do for another in the name of Jesus Christ.

Trench Ministry -The uncomfortable and difficult side of Christian ministry.

Ministry- The spiritual work of self-less action by Christians that is connected to evangelism.

Reason #2 not to quit ministry:

Trench ministry produces the greatest rewards because it mirrors Christ ministry.

Chapter 3: Double Down

Increasing your prayer life can make a dramatic change in your ministry.

1 Kings 18:38, NIV
"Then the fire of the Lord fell, and consumed the burnt sacrifice, and the wood, and the stones, and the dust, and licked up the water that was in the trench."

1 Kings 19:9, NKJV
"And there he went into a cave, and spent the night in that place; and behold, the word of the Lord came to him, and He said to him, "What are you doing here, Elijah?"

■■■

God often startles me, in my journey as a minister, that if I am not careful I begin to love the teachings of His word more than I love the Person of His word. I begin to love religion more than the relationship. The story of Elijah is such a powerful story for ministers. Especially since in the book of James it says, *"Elijah was a man with like passions as we" (James 5:17).* I always cherished that phrase because it reminds us that God has always used ordinary people to do extraordinary things. The great preacher E.E. Cleveland was quoted saying, "I have seen God do so much with so little, that I now believe He can do anything, with anyone, including me." There is nothing special about the vessel, except what God puts in it. My job is simply to be available and willing. But often it is my willingness that gets me in trouble, surprisingly. Because as a minister, I want to be used so much that I focus on the "doing" instead of the "being". And it is when we forget 'who we are in Christ', that the 'what we do for Christ' becomes convoluted.

Elijah had just finished "doing" a lot for God. He was used to literally turn back an entire nation to God using an alter and a trench. But after this great feat of faith we find Elijah running for his life away from Jezebel. I mean this guy had seen God do some stupid amazing things. He was fed three times a day by ravens, spoke truth to a powerful king and lived, literally was teleported through walls, ran faster than a chariot downhill in the rain and mud, watched oil and flour multiply, and not to mention actually with his own two eyes, saw fire come down from heaven from God Himself. But yet we find Elijah hiding in a cave because he is afraid of Jezebel. This just goes to show us that it really doesn't matter what God uses us to do in our ministry, depression and trench experiences can happen to the best of us.

After we saw the moving of God to feed the homeless with only a few pots of food, when we saw him provide the money for that building project, when we received that check from that unknown sender, when He restored our children to health, when our loans were forgiven, when we preached a message that brought thousands to Christ, when we felt His Spirit lift us up and break strong-holds, but yet we still find ourselves questioning our call and hiding from the enemy.

The cave of Elijah is where I have too often been. And surprisingly enough I usually find myself there as soon as I compete some great task for Christ. After digging the trench for God's glory, I then crawl into it and hide from those who stand against me. It is the low after the high. The roller coaster rides of ministry that once you go up, you seem to come down. Saturday night after I have preached and ministered is always when the temptations come on the strongest. And this is when we must focus our mind on how important it is to "be in Christ" then just to "do for Christ". What Elijah learns and what God is still teaching me, is that when you are in the cave afraid for your life, double down and hear his voice.

Elijah forgot who God was, he knew what God could do but had lost sight of His person. For me this happens when I look at my relationship as a practice instead of a process. A practice is set and doesn't change, what you put in will determine what will come out. But a process works to bring the needed results after some time, it is a journey. God has us in His process and on His journey and who can know His ways. Let me say something that may shock you; sometimes answered prayers are the worst thing to happen in our relationship with God. When I say "answered" I mean prayers that get the answer that you want. Just think about it. Isn't it true that whenever God answers our prayers the way we want; we naturally try to rationalize how it could have happened without God. We immediately belittle the miracle. It is almost like our rational minds refuse to let us believe in the miracle. Even though we have told ourselves we believe we almost instinctively want to find another reason for the answer besides God. Okay so you say you never do that? But why did you neglect to pray even after you got the blessing you wanted? Or why is it you have to remind yourself every so often that you need to do better in your relationship with God? I think it happens when we lose sight of who He is and what prayer is all about. Prayer is about a constant intentional connection with God, not just when He does what we want.

Our spiritual connection is not necessarily strengthened by answered prayers and big miracles. As humans we tend to forget that it was God who answered our prayers when we sporadically connect to Him simply to get what we want out of Him. But when we remain connected to the source of our strength and as we learn who He is in the midst of our suffering, during the answered or unanswered prayers, we find something better than the answer. In the worst of our lives we clamor and claw for something, someone larger than the answer we seek, we find Him.

Our search for God leads us to find out who we really are.

Because even in the unanswered prayers we can praise God because we've learned how to trust His plan above our own comfort. The unanswered prayers taught us who we were apart from our own will. We were able to learn about His will. Sometimes prayer and connection are less about the ending and more about the journey. It becomes about how God is shaping our character through the valleys and in the trench. I always have to remember that God has me on a journey that calls me to follow Jesus. This is not a light Sabbath/Sunday school statement. It means that I literally observe His life and realize that if the world hated Him, it will hate me.

Trials

Only as I stay connected to Jesus can I conduct my daily lift of the cross and follow Him to die to self. He fills me up and becomes the God in me, the mind of Christ takes over. So, when trials come, the trial becomes a part of my journey instead of just a bump in the road. The bump is actually intentional. It is not for me to decide if the obstacle was placed intentionally by God or if God chose to use it to grow me. Instead I have confidence that as I am walking with Him, even this will be worked out for good. And it is good because I am holding on to the One who is good.

If you are like me when obstacles come, stressors invade your peace, or life throws you a curve ball it brings us discomfort. It causes us to become more cynical or more serious in our prayer life. We may even get angry at God for allowing such a thing to happen to us. These are moments we all face, and it is important to meet these emotions, understanding the reason for the trenches. These problems are a part of the suffering that was promised to us, they are expected on this journey. The trench is there so our character may be perfected. The trench is there so that we can double down and recognize that God is in the trench.

So, when things are going well in my life, I am happy, but I am not naive. I know that life is not luxury, so I am thankful for the pause, but in anticipation of the next trial. In fact, I begin to look forward to the next trial because in my suffering it perfects my character. I need this character perfected because I am kingdom bound.

You see not everyone wants their character perfected because not everyone is kingdom bound. So that is why I can never compare my situation to anyone else, because I know nothing of their journey. I just trust in the plan and journey that God has for me. The wicked may seem like they are being blessed, but what they have is their only reward. We are not going to the same place. But if I am disconnected from Jesus at times, I can forget and start feeling depressed. I begin to think "woe is me" if I was focused on Christ I would praise Him for the trench.

In my life there have been times when I only fervently prayed when I needed something from God. Maybe I lost an important piece of paper, wanted a good grade on a test, or something worse like financial issues or a family member was sick. I would spend as much time as I could in agony begging God to answer my prayers. Sometimes making bargains with God that if He only got me out of this mess I would stop doing a certain sin. We know this rhythm of Christianity all too well. But look at what kind of relationship I created for myself and God. I placed Him in a position as a tyrant or genie that I must rub the right way to get my desired outcome. Some people don't like God, not because of who He is, but because of who they have made Him to be.

Now let's reimagine how this could go. Imagine instead I have lived a life of connection during the good or the bad. When an unexpected trial comes we still feel frantic and we still will pray more earnestly but something is different. I am not playing catch up in my relationship with God. He is not a distant friend but someone that we have been in constant connection with. It isn't far to run to Jesus because we would have been walking with Him already. The difference is peace and presence. Peace that I feel in my mind because of where I have placed Jesus in relation to my problems. Let us make this clear, no matter what, Jesus is always there nearby, it is our own thoughts that make Him seem distant. It is our sin that has separated us from God (Isaiah 58:1) and this causes us to not hear Him clearly. As we live a life focused and aware of His presence this becomes the new normal for our lives. Being aware of Jesus' presence regularly, will allow for peace during the seemingly irregular.

And what I have noticed is that when I see my life as a journey to get me to the Kingdom, I place trials in a different perspective. Not only because of the goal but because of the God who is with me through it all.

Connection

This type of mindset towards life requires what I call the informality of our prayer lives. If we are being honest it is extremely hard to stay connected. Our minds often wonders, even the short few minutes of our morning prayers. Our mind is easily distracted by our own lives and needs. Jesus however was able to remain in constant connection with the father while He walked the earth. One thing that Jesus had that we must learn is a discomfort in disconnection. I think about when my daughter was an infant, she would get hungry after waking up from a long nap. We never have to guess what she wanted or what time it was, because her shrieks and screams would let us know. Her belly is empty, and she wants to eat and eat NOW! My wife and I would rush to get her food and fill that need because of her cry. Her desperation and little baby tears moved us to action to give her the milk her little belly so desired. Our desire for God must become the same way. Instead of tears of the trench, let's cry to be filled by the source of our strength. God wants to teach us how to stay in constant connection so that even when we do not get what we want we are still satisfied.

The miracle of prayer is not simply getting the answer I desire; the miracle is finding Jesus in my quest for the blessing. Some want Jesus for the help He promises to provide for them, others just want Jesus. My daughter is a toddler now and she cries for my attention. When we drop her off at the daycare that is one of the most painful times for both of us. When I hand her over to the teacher, my baby immediately cries, and I see the pleas in her eyes as tears stream down her face. She cries to me not because she is hungry, tired, or needs a diaper change but because she wants to stay with me. She craves our connection and disconnection to her is uncomfortable. I hope she reads this when she is a teenager. With God, we are the toddlers, and we should never grow out of a desire for connection. Remember, Jesus stayed connected to the Father not because it would relieve his physical pain but because it sustained His spirit.

On the cross Jesus dies from a broken heart as the weight of the world's sin is placed on his conscience. He dies because the disconnection is too great, His Father has "forsaken Him" (Matthew 27:46). This disconnection that Jesus felt on the cross because of our sin is the feeling that we have learned to exist in. The separation, the disconnection for us has become normal. Millions of children of God operate on a daily basis without feeling any discomfort for being disconnected from the life giver. We are too comfortable living with the sin that separates and self that dictates. We must pray that our normal becomes the abnormal and that Christ's normal becomes our normal. We want to feel a need to remain in Him. We want to yearn for the still small voice amidst the chaos and recognize it as an expectation. We must pray to become like Jesus, where we crave connection and disconnection becomes abnormal.

No matter how much we prepare we will always end up in the Elijah caves of our lives. In those trench experiences we must be reintroduced to God. The text says a still small voice was heard. God will speak to you. He will show us who we are and who He is. But know that the process of ministry is less about what you do and more about who you become. The becoming will give you a reason to do and turn your attention away from your problems.

Intercession

Another major part of our prayer life must be intercession. When we commit to pray for others, our problems are not as important. Remember ministry is about selflessness. In Paul's letter to the Ephesians he famously outlines the pieces needed for the armor of God. At the end of this beautiful description of God's armor, Paul says, *"Praying always with all prayer and supplication in the Spirit and watching thereunto with all perseverance and supplication for all saints" (Ephesians 6:18).* A part of our warfare involves praying for others. We often forget to pray for the saints because the saints have beat on us. We would rather just mope or wait for things to just work themselves out, then involve God and give some half-hearted prayers. But this happens because our lives have become so invested in ourselves and our own interest. If we would be in a habit of intercession for others we would see our problems in a different light.

Many people wonder "why me?" when they face trials, but we usually do not say "why not me?" When we consider the lives of others many times our problems are not as major. As my dad used to always say, "It could always be worse." And that is so true, however we often still don't feel comforted. The comfort must come from your own choice to be selfless. Yes, in the midst of your trial force yourself to pray for someone else.

Like dad said, someone else will always be in a worse situation than you. And there are those times between trials that you feel blessed and have no complaints. The temptation again is to keep praying for yourself, to be content with the happy connection between you and God. I want to suggest that we practice joining others in their trench. We learn how to become the shoulders that others need to lean on. We often complain that no one is there for us when we haven't practiced being there for someone else.

This idea of intercession while in the trench, connects perfectly with our task as ministers to seek and save the lost. This commission is never turned off. Imagine, Jesus on the cross, by far the worst possible trial of any human's life, and yet He still witnessed and saved the thief on the cross. Paul being shipwrecked, Peter in prison, disciples being tortured never saw their current situation as an excuse not to intercede for someone else. When we have this type of attitude in every facet of our lives we spoil the darts the enemy throws our way. Our faith in Christ and for Christ bats them away. We can freely do this because we realize it is not all about us, there is more to the story then our current predicament. This is what Elijah fails to realize when he runs from Jezebel. He thinks that He is all alone and that everything revolves around his situation.

Elijah forgets that God was not just using him to save others, but God worked through Elijah to also save Elijah. That is why after all the mighty acts, God speaks forth in the still small voice. He is a personal God who loves us and is concerned for us. But He also wants us to realize that there is always more to the story then what we can see. If we would simply focus on His voice and let Him worry about the rest, we may see a different viewpoint. We may then finally realize that God called us to the discomfort of trench ministry in order to save us. That His calling on our life is His ministry towards us. Elijah thought he was the only one but found out he was one of five thousand. His message to Elijah and to us is, 'I love you enough to use you, because I need to use you to save you.'

The fear of depression and the burden of intercession keep me from quitting ministry. I realize that I am here to be saved and help save others. I pray to allow God to let me see things from His perspective. I want to be able to stay in connection with Him so that I am in tune with the needs around me. When we begin to pray for Jesus and intercede for others instead of simply offering a laundry list of wants, our perspective begins to change. As we become like Him, we begin to think like Him. God and the gospel is about what can be given. *"For God so loved, that He gave..." (John 3:16).* Only when we have the mind of Christ can we think in this way.

▪ Something to Try ▪

Try two things.

1) Begin to study to be fed for yourself. Rediscover who Jesus is and pray daily to die to self. Pray again for His Heart and Mind. Find Jesus.

2) Begin to intercede. Jump into someone else's trench and begin to act like Jesus. Let His mind change yours.

Reason #3 not to quit ministry:

Ministry is to save you to save others.

Chapter 4: Don't Call Saul

Ministry is about the people, even the difficult ones that have lost their savor.

1 Sam 24:3,4, NKJV
"So, he came to the sheepfolds by the road, where there was a cave; and Saul went in to attend to his needs. (David and his men were staying in the recesses of the cave.)"

1 Sam 26:5, KJV
"And David arose, and came to the place where Saul had pitched: and David beheld the place where Saul lay, and Abner the son of Ner the captain of his host: and Saul lay in the trench, and the people pitched round about him."

■■■

Okay I know, I know, in the text David is in the cave and Saul is in the trench. But it still serves to represent the same trench experience we have been discussing. David and his men have been running for their lives from King Saul. David is one of my favorite Bible characters besides Joshua of course. David was the preamble to Robin Hood, Luke Skywalker, and Batman. He is one of those noble super heroes in the Bible fighting against a crazy tyrant for justice and peace.

As a young minister I cannot help but see myself in that cave with David every time I read that story. Although I am not running for my life or battling an insane king I can relate to feelings of fear and those I call, "the Sauls". These "Sauls" are those individuals you will meet on your ministry journey that have been sent to throw a monkey wrench in your conflict resolution strategy and leadership training. These individuals or groups do not play by any rules or have any regard for regulations. These are those that lurk at the bottom of the trench to catch you off guard. Now before you accuse me of name calling, I will be the first to admit I have fit into "the Saul" category a few times. Let me further explain "the Sauls" by continuing the story.

King Saul is literally trying to kill his son's best friend, a man who has made his kingdom safer (i.e. Goliath is dead), and a righteous man (i.e. Little David play on your harp). The only reason for Saul's anger is because of his own sin and the subsequent jealousy that David would take over the kingdom one day. And let's not forget that Saul is lucky to even be King in the first place because this whole kingship wasn't even God's idea. But what makes Saul even more crazy in my opinion is even after David spares his life in the cave, two chapters later Saul is back trying to kill David again. And when David spares his life yet again, his response is almost identical to that in chapter 24. This guy had some serious problems. Now I understand the power of jealousy just like the next guy, but we all know that Saul was dealing with more than pride at this point. The Bible says that the Spirit of God had left him. Now that is a serious statement and should be a very scary one as well.

The reality is that some sitting next to us in church have had the Spirit of God leave them. They are in the soup kitchen dishing out food, leading Sabbath school or Sunday school, they are on your ministry staff, and they plan your youth group trips. There are people that we interact with every single day who may fall into the category called "the Sauls". Now let me be clear again that I am not promoting a witch hunt or name calling. My definition of being a "Saul" is not that someone deems you as acting different or odd, what I am talking about are people who literally have grieved the Spirit of God or are letting the enemy use them for a time. These individuals do not have to be foaming at the mouth and speaking in a demonic deep voice. There are people who you may know very well that can easily slip into "the Saul" category because of unresolved sin in their life. The Bible says by their fruit you shall know them, and it also admonishes us to be wise as serpents and harmless as doves (Matthew 7:16, 10:16). So, there is a sense of spiritual discernment that you must carry within ministry.

You will find yourself in arguments that you have no business being in because you're arguing with someone who is not reasonable. Remember also, as you read this that some people may actually have medical conditions or a chemical imbalance thus it is important not to diagnose or predetermine. There are more people than one may think in the church suffering from a type of mental disorder. Many people in ministry who have been around a lot of people know exactly what I am talking about. We do not label people, but instead we hear from the Spirit as to identify and discern spirits that show up in people. Because even so, God has called us to ministry, among and at times even to "the Sauls".

When you are in ministry mode you will find individuals, who may play the part well but in truth they are struggling with some serious cosmic forces. The important thing to remember is that all of us are susceptible of falling into the "Saul" category. Anytime we let pride, anger, or even fear get in the way of our judgment we are letting in demonic attributes to rule us. We never want to be on the side that is fighting against God. This alone should drive us to stay connected so that we can be prayed up enough to identify those who are against God's plans. God will give spiritual discernment as we pray for wisdom and pray for those who often drive us deeper into the trench.

The Woes

In my short time in ministry I have been called outside my name, lied on, verbally abused, publicly disrespected, and even had a woman put her fist in my face. Now that last one is a story I need to share one day. I have even had times when I went to greet someone, and they stared in my face without even flinching to shake my hand. Now by no stretch of the imagination am I perfect nor, will I start defending myself on every instance, but never should such actions be warranted to anyone. I have had colleagues and friends who have gone through much worse abuse, physically and emotionally towards them and their family. And let us remember those who face untold sufferings in our mission fields around the world. No matter the magnitude of the abuse these things are serious and do affect us in various ways.

I realize that in many cases I underwent abuse by those I was sent to serve. Looking at the life of Jesus, I believe I shared good company. It really takes more than just prayer to get over these situations. Prayer, coupled with counseling, conflict resolution, lengthy vacations, spiritual discernment, and then more prayer is all appropriate. For at least one of my churches, I suffered from a form of PTSD. Every time I traveled there or even set foot in the building my heart would beat faster, and my breathing would quicken. And as soon as I drove away I would immediately calm down. Some would say I needed to look in the mirror to see my faults that brought on all this negative energy. I would say that what I experienced actually pales in comparison to the emotional fears and feelings I have heard from my colleagues around the country. Most cases were little about blame, and more of receiving the brunt of someone's misplaced anger.

In ministry it's easy to be the punching bag even if you are just the messenger. I remember one member calling me after a sermon I preached saying they were offended by my message. I try hard not to preach against people or to a particular incident from the pulpit and this sermon was no exception, but many times people fight hard against conviction. As God told Samuel, *"It is not you they have rejected, they have rejected me as their king"* (1 Sam 8:7 NIV). And that's just it, as long as you are following God you can be confident in what you do, remember you are God's representative. Some things we cannot take personal because we remember there is a spiritual battle. This also means that we must be willing to admit when we are wrong and seek peace where peace is possible.

#TrenchChronicles

It was the very first board meeting of my career and I was extremely nervous. Many people don't realize that in theology school we are taught to be just that, theologians, we get very little training to be Pastors. I think this has since begun to change at my alma mater but back then we only had one class on how to run a church. Yes, we were supposed to spend a semester being mentored under a Pastor, but many times that still wasn't enough.

I sat at the head of the table, palms perspiring as I rustled through my notes. The members slowly began to file in as I cordially greeted each of them, hoping this would give me some brownie points for the meeting. I had heard the horror stories about difficult members, arguments in the meetings, challenging the Pastor, even heard some meetings ending in fist fights. Those early childhood memories of dad saying that board meetings were just that, "boring meetings". Memories of him, as first elder, coming home after board meetings late and exhausted, haunted me now. I remember seeing them go into that conference room not to return for hours. I never knew what went on in those meetings, but it didn't look fun. Come to think of it, this board meeting possibly was about to be my first one I had ever attended. I had only been a junior deacon and head usher, and I served on the nominating committee once.

I passed out the agendas and called the meeting to order. Two hours later the meeting was thankfully over but the meeting had validated all of my fears. For the entire meeting one of the board members had been riding my case, quoting the Church Manual and Roberts Rules of Order the entire time. Afterwards he pulled me aside and continued to school me on the countless violations I committed during the meeting. I told him I was doing my best and would love for him to give me some pointers for the next meeting. We met at his house and mostly spent the entire time discussing his grievances and other political moves he wanted to make. At the next meeting he had increased his critiques. This time he was louder and more forceful than before. It got so unbearable that I was basically unable to get a word in to continue the meeting. He was taking over my meeting and probably hoping to take over the church. I started to panic as his words began to run together and the room became tense. Never had I been in a situation like this nor had I trained for this, I wanted to get up and leave. But instead I prayed, and the Spirit of God settled me and gave me strength. I sat up in my chair and began to speak firmly and louder, but this only aggravated the man and he began to match my volume. "This was not about to become a shouting match" I thought. So, I did the only thing I could think to do, and I banged my hand on the table and said "Please be quiet! Anyone else who would like to speak must raise their hand." Startled, he slowly raised his hand. I put my head down and said, "As the board chairman I will not be calling on your hand. Now can we continue with the meeting please?", half asking but mainly pleading. As soon as the words left my lips he and his wife stood up, gathered their things, and said something to the effect that if this was how I ran the church they would not be back. And they never did come back. I never saw that man again until an awkward moment at a conference convention where we both were washing our hands in the restroom. Pleasantries were exchanged but that was it.

I will never forget that story for two reasons. For one, I remember how the other members looked at me when I stood up to the man. I could feel a sigh of relief and tell that they just needed someone to show leadership. But also, because it motivated me to always be prayed up and to become the best in my field. I realize even today that many times people will leave the church or your organization who had no business being there in the first place. If the spirit of the enemy is in them and the spirit of God is in you, all you must do is pray them uncomfortable. When we pray against the evil spirit and not against the people we begin to see something amazing happen. Either the evil spirit will be cast out of them or in their resistance of conviction they will leave with the enemy's spirit. This is what I feel happened that day. There was no way for the two spirits to exist in the same room and prayer not cast out the evil spirit.

Since then I have learned just a few more things on how to curb such a situation if it happened again. However, at the end of the day dealing with 'Sauls' is really the Spirit's specialty. You have to be connected because each situation is different. There are times to engage and times to leave things alone, so let the Spirit lead you as you review these suggestions below.

Dealing with Difficult People

1. Document everything – this goes without much needed explanation except when I say everything, I mean everything! There may be laws against recording people in certain settings, but you can still type or write on a running document you keep as to what occurred in your conversations.

2. Visit, visit, visit – Most people will cut you slack if you have built a relationship with them.

3. Discuss your ideas - Never assume people share your same

views but be prepared to stand firm and make a case for your opinion.

4. Don't chase rabbits – many discussions and questions are just traps. Learn to do like Jesus and just be silent. I know it sounds bad, but sometimes just not answering them and looking at them changes minds.

5. Take your time – never let people rush you. It is best to get it right then to rush a wrong decision just to please people. In the end you will end up losing.

6. "Can we try this?" - anytime people know that a decision is temporary they are more apt to go along.

7. Don't be afraid to say you don't know – if you come off as a "know-it-all" you will have to know it all and you don't. So, it is best just to admit that you don't know and that you will find out.

8. Sit down with people – this has worked wonders for me. Just be straight up with people and find out what their problem is. You will be surprised when you get to the bottom. You will have your counselor hat on by the end of the meeting, believe me.

9. Be firm. You are a child of the King – never question the power He has given you. The majority of people do not want to be on the wrong side of leadership. As long as you are filled with integrity and being truthful you have much power on your side.

10. Ask for Grace – remind people that you are human and often make mistakes. You need some benefit of the doubt extended to you at times too. Be sincere.

There have been times when I was really bold and wanted to sit down to address issues with difficult people. Then there have also been times when I just wanted to leave that person alone. The times I sat down with people all ended very well, but it was after much prayer. My prayer is usually this:

Lord please give me Your patience and Your passion. Give us both the mind of Christ and the heart of God. Open our eyes so that we can see and open our ears that we may hear. Shower us with Your Spirit. Amen.

Never has God disappointed. Pray a prayer on who you should sit down with because some people God may just want you to leave to Him. Not every battle is going to be won nor should every battle be fought. Even Jesus picked His battles. But ultimately remember that we fight not against flesh and blood. We are literal warriors in the great controversy and just like we never know when we encounter angels, we never know when we are encountering demons, so stay prayed up. The good news is, if the devil is attacking it means he is scared and as ministers we can always work with that.

Reason #4 not to quit ministry:

The enemy knows you're on to something great.

Chapter 5: Pitfalls

The very thing that keeps causing you to stumble is the very thing God is using to save you.

Proverbs 22:14, KJV
"The mouth of strange women is a deep pit: He that is abhorred of Jehovah shall fall therein."

Judges 16:20, NIV
"Then she called, "Samson, the Philistines are upon you!" He awoke from his sleep and thought, "I'll go out as before and shake myself free." But he did not know that the LORD had left him."

■■■

Lust is one of those areas that whether you are a minister, Pastor, or a holier than thou saint, you will have to tackle. A point I sure wish had been made known to me before going into ministry. It seems that most of my pastor colleagues and ministry workers tend to struggle with lust in some form. Some have even said that with the call of God the devil automatically sends the demon of lust. I am no exception to the rule. I have struggled with this since I was a boy. The temptations heightened even while going into full-time pastoral ministry. The devil has tempted me with pornography, sexual promiscuity, and addictive lust. Sadly, and ashamedly I have fallen in these areas.

When you have a specific sin problem and you do not address it immediately, you develop habits and even addictions. These habits become so entrenched in your life that they become a part of your life, even normal. The guilt slowly begins to fade away and you see sin from a totally different vantage point. You have crossed over into the hypocrite camp and it starts to be how you exist. There is one thing to have a sin that you struggle with, and another to have a sin that you learn to live with. I found myself rationalizing sin, I knew that it was wrong, but the Spirit was faded out. I had convinced myself that this was just who I was and there was no reason to change.

The merciful thing about God is that He will let you think you're fooling Him. He may even bless you with the ability to still do powerful ministry. The reason I believe He allows this is that the Word is still His Word whether the messenger is weak, the Word is still powerful. He also will show His power by using the most foolish of the world to deliver His Word (1 Corinthians 1:27). He will sometimes shield our sin in order to bless the people. However, this can only go on for so long until you literally cannot hear God's voice anymore. There comes a point in time when our sin literally begins to separate us from God. Praise God that His love is still there even in the midst of our foolishness. But that feeling of sinning and repenting and then praying to be forgiven again for something I know I am going to do again, well that gets old really quick. At some point in time we have to fall on our face and admit we cannot do it anymore. We have to give it all to Jesus and let Him fix our problem. The trouble is I did that, I gave my lust to Him, and He didn't take it away. In fact, I began to question what "giving your whole heart to Jesus" even means. "What really is true conversion?" I would cry out to God. What does it even look like because I am preaching to others, but you will not take this addiction from me. My lack of guilt had turned to anger with God.

Once I got married I knew that it was time to let this lust problem go. I was not naïve; I knew that marriage would not solve anything. But after marriage I knew that I was doing better than I had before. It helped that I married a beautiful and Godly woman who knew before and knows now all of my pitfalls and yet still loves me unconditionally. I believe that God's gift of marriage really began to answer some of my questions of Him. It taught me what "giving my whole heart" actually meant. It showed me that I had never opened my heart up to love anyone but myself. It had always been about my wants, needs, and desires and never about His. I was too selfish to give my heart to anyone let alone Christ. It showed up clear in my marriage when my actions spoke louder than my constant, "I love you's". I realized that self stood in the way of giving my God and my wife the happiness they deserved. I had spent so many years faking my walk with God and my purity that it was almost like I was incapable of truly loving anyone other than me. I knew I liked them, but love meant that I would have to forsake my own wants for the sake of theirs. And truthfully, I was not ready to do that.

I read a book by my friend Jason O'Rourke called "Sexuology" that really opened my eyes to the psychological and chemical damage I had done to myself over the years. Damage that almost made it emotionally impossible for me to love anyone other than myself. When I began to see that self-love stems from Satan Himself I knew that God would have to totally rearrange me entirely. God will use a number of areas to rescue us from sin and sometimes He uses a miracle, His Word, preaching, friends, support groups, or counseling. For me it has taken every last one of those to bring me to the place I am today. God showed me that the dirt I do, or did in the dark was never in the dark, it was always in the light. You see many addicts have people in their life they are ashamed to show their addiction to. For example, many drug addicts I meet will try to hide their problem from me when they discover I am a Pastor. So, it becomes second nature to hide your problems, which of course started in the garden with Adam and Eve.

So, for me it was easy to hide my lust from my parents, church, friends, and now even my wife. But what God showed me is that I was holding those individuals in a higher regard than Him. You see I felt I was getting over and getting by even if I slipped up on occasion. At least no one found out right? But the entire time God was right there, and He saw, He knew what I did and what I was thinking when I did it. So, in essence I either didn't care if He knew or was saying He wasn't relevant. Thankfully He is a loving God who truly knows my heart and has showed me endless mercy.

Each time I messed up I hid it from everyone else but God and that was okay with me. I was holding other people's opinions of me over God's opinion of me. I actually loved my wife more than I loved God. Because if you keep hurting someone and then say after you do it, "Oh, it is fine, they will forgive me." Do you really love that person and value them? That is exactly how I was treating God, I was using Him, playing Him for a fool.

God used a number of things in my life to come to this profound yet simple conclusion. One of which was when I was asked by the director of the Dare to Dream 3ABN Christian television network to host a program called "Pure Choices", I knew God was up to something. This program probably did more therapy for me than it did for the viewers. It allowed me the avenue to work through my issues and share my journey in a real authentic way. I know that this is a hard subject for us to talk about especially with the "perfect" view that people have of pastors and church leaders. But I do not know why people put such unrealistic high exceptions on us. Pastors, especially, are the ones attacked the most. And if we cannot talk about our struggles openly then it perpetuates the very temptation to keep it a secret. I am no different, or more holy than any other man. My calling is more holy, my work is more holy, my office is holy, but I am still just a man.

I love how the King James words James 5:17, *"Elijah was a man subject to like passions as we are..."*. I love that the Bible is authentic and real. We often fail to read it like that, instead we place these prophets and kings on pedestals, when in reality they were broken sinners just like us. The truth is, sometimes I want to quit ministry because I feel I am not holy enough, but then God reminds me that none are righteous. We all have fallen short and will keep on falling short. The biggest difference for me today is that instead of running to evil, evil has to chase me. I am actively living the "resisting" and "drawing nigh" principle from James 4:8. The key in all of this is to remember that we are still no match for the enemy alone. As soon as I take my eyes off of Jesus I begin to fall, no matter how many victories I have conquered. Lust is different than an addiction to cigarettes because cigarettes are not supposed to be smoked in the first place, but lust comes from a natural desire for sex and intimacy. It is one of the most common vices in the church but the one least spoken about. I have accepted that I will be fighting this battle for the rest of my life, but I gain peace knowing that God's grace is sufficient.

Some think Paul's "thorn in the flesh" was his eyesight but I like to think just maybe he struggled with lust too. "Three times I pleaded with the Lord to take it away from me. But he said to me,

'My grace is sufficient for you, for my power is made perfect in weakness.' Therefore, I will boast all the more gladly about my weaknesses, so that Christ's power may rest on me" (1 Corinthians 12:8-9). Paul was able to boast in weakness because he knew God would strengthen him.

The Other Side of Victory

It has most definitely gotten easier, but I still cannot take any chances. I have learned my triggers and how to stay prayed up each day. An old man said that his body may have changed with age, but he still has the same eyes. I praise God that each day He delivers me from temptations and sin. I thank Him for a wonderful wife and daughter. I thank God for victories and for second, third, fourth, and so many chances. I thank Him for allowing me to make a decision to live for Him even if I do fall, He picks me back up. Even in this state of thankfulness I know that there are many people that still struggle with this temptation. I also realize that there are people that I have hurt along the way in my journey to wholeness. And there are colleagues of mine who did things that they were unable to recover from and are now out of the ministry. This is a serious thing, that if not for God's mercy and grace, who knows where I would be right now.

No matter if you are wanting to quit ministry because of a sin you committed that you think disqualifies you from ministry, realize that this is a part of trench ministry. Trench ministry is being in that pit of temptation, sometimes even falling, but finding God and falling back in love with Him. This moment in your life is a part of the ministry journey that God is creating. He is going to provide for you a way of escape even if it seems there is no way out. I want to encourage you that if God has called you to ministry, He will bring you through ministry. God can restore us to His work in due time. Do not think that you have gone so far that God cannot bring you back. I have seen it happen with countless ministers. Keep your hand in Christ's and pray for a hatred for sin. God will hear your cry and He will restore you.

#TrenchChronicles

It was late. The house was quiet, and my wife had already fallen asleep. I ever so carefully pulled back the sheet and comforter on our King size bed trying not to wake her. I paused as the rhythm of her breathing seemed to change but it receded back to quiet breathing that only could mean she was sleep. I slipped on my house shoes and reached for the squeaky door. Every turn of the nob I winced as I made sure she was still asleep. After a number of slow maneuvers, I was finally on the other side and in the hallway. As I arrived in the living room I safely turned on the light. I looked back at the master bedroom door, thankful in the darkness I had missed all the noisy obstacles along the way. She was still sleep, and I had hours of freedom ahead of me. I quietly sat down on the couch making myself comfortable. All through the day my mind had been going crazy anticipating this moment. It was finally time. No one to bother me. No one to interrupt me. No one to know about my guilty pleasure. I ever so quietly turned on the TV, slid in the DVD, and began to play my Play station four newly purchased DC game all night. As the sun began to come up I had already slipped back into the bed without a peep from my wife. Just as my eyes began to close, she woke up and stretched. She leaned over and kissed me and said, "Good morning dear! I have a surprise for you." One of my eyes opened and I could tell she saw the redness around my pupils. "What kind of surprise?" I asked half asleep. "Well", she said, "today is your day off and I want to let you use the TV all day without any interruption to play your new video game." I could not believe it. I just laid there and I could feel her smiling over me...she knew, she knew.

The Easy Beset

You can substitute whatever your vice may be in this story. No matter what your pitfall may be, whether it is something you do not think is that bad or something you know is bad, remember that these types of trenches stand in the way of your relationship with God. These temptations can cause you to think worse of ministry than it really may be. You can be drawn away from God and even to a place where you could care less. So, remember that God is always with you. It is not about resisting temptation for others, it is about retaining your connection with God. Satan will try to do anything to keep you from doing ministry. A part of God's ministry towards us is to be with us during the hard times and to provide ways of escape. Sometimes we make it hard for God to find those ways of escape, but remember that nothing is too hard for Him. He already foresaw that you would make that mistake and wrote a plan eons ago to rescue you.

One of the scariest aspects of ministry is attempting to do it without the power of God. Satan knows what will trip us up and he knows what will keep us disconnected from the source of power. Even knowing this we still constantly slip up time and time again. As I mentioned earlier, it is easy to develop a feeling of comfort with the sin and find a way to operate in ministry with half power. We never truly learn all that God can do through us because we continue to only give Him half.

In Sampson's story he had given his soul and secret to the temptress to the point where he had fooled himself. When his captors came in he thought he could just get up like before and defeat the enemy, however he did not realize that the Spirit of God had left him. It makes me shudder just writing this because can you imagine how insane that must have felt. To literally have the form of godliness but lack the power (2 Timothy 3:5). To be wearing a robe on Sunday or Sabbath morning with no Word able to come out of your lips because the Spirit has left you. Building a community center or starting a community initiative by your own strength without any vision from God. These are scary thoughts, but people operate like this week after week.

Our church has been high jacked by ministers who refuse to address the weakness they choose to live with. It is this fear, the fear of operating without His Spirit and power that has kept me uncomfortable and repentant in my struggle. This is what has kept me disturbed and running back to Him, and He knows it. God knows that for some of us it took the ministry to save us. Because without the constant need for His power, without the responsibility to represent Him, and speak His words, we would probably have nothing to do with Him. We would continue to live half powered lives and continue to sin. But I thank God, every time I want to quit ministry I remember that He called me to ministry to save me. If it wasn't for my particular call to minister as a Pastor, each week preparing sermons, each week standing in the gap, and witnessing for His name, I would be out in the streets somewhere. But each week I am forced to my knees to run back to the cross and cling to my Savior and weep at His feet. Each week I learn a little more about his unfettered love for me. Each week I discover God, He knocks, and I answer. Each week I learn how to worship Him. The author said, "Sexual sin is, at its core, a worship disorder. That's why our search for true spiritual intimacy can get us involved in some pretty extreme, destructive stuff, sexually speaking. G. K. Chesterton is said to have once remarked, "Every man who knocks on the door of a brothel is looking for God" (Hide or Seek by John Freeman).

■ Something to Try ■

Take time to really learn who you are and your relationship with God. Take time to attend counseling or join a support group. Use a prayer journal, prayer wall, post up scripture texts, find an accountability partner, etc. Be intentional and let God stop the cycle of pitfalls in your life.

Reason #5 not to quit ministry:

The call to ministry is saving you.

Chapter 6: Jump. No Fear.

God has given you strength beyond what you are using. Do not let the devil get you down and you miss out on all that God is trying to do through you.

1 Chronicles 11:22, KJV
"Benaiah the son of Jehoiada, the son of a valiant man of Kabzeel, who had done many acts; he slew two lionlike men of Moab: also, he went down and slew a lion in a pit in a snowy day."

■■■

It was the summer after my High School graduation. While many of my counterparts were BBQ'n at pool parties, enjoying their last summer before adulthood, I found myself beating the scorched streets of a town called Bakersfield. Legend has it, that there, under the dry summer heat you can fry an egg on the pavement. I never tried but if my feet count, they sure fried that day. But I pressed on, door after door, house after house with my bag of Christian books over my shoulder and walkie-talkie securely fastened to my belt. I was a summer Bible book evangelist, or colporteurs as we called ourselves. About twelve to fourteen other students around my age with four college age leaders descended upon this city for four weeks. Our mission was to spread the gospel and fund our education by disseminating as many of our Christian mega books as humanly possible.

Colporteur work was actually a great endeavor that taught me so many crucial life lessons and challenged my relationship with Christ. I will always attribute this summer to my first real encounter with ministry. It was a fairly rigorous program that required prayer, focus, and a go-getter mentality. The first night we arrived was spent memorizing our canvass or script we would use at the doors of the homes. I had just graduated the day before and I was still in this "I'm done; can I have fun now?" type mindset. But now having to memorize something felt way too much like school. I tried hard to focus but could not recite the litany of words correct enough to impress the leaders. Others around me picked it up quickly and even were able to go out for the first time that night.

Although it was never overtly stated, we all knew there was a subtle competition to see who could sell the most books. And for me this was extremely personal for at least three main reasons. My father owned a retail business and I expected myself to be this natural salesman, I was the only one who was planning to be a Pastor, and well because I was the only black kid there, I had to represent. So that night, not being able to go out and start this ministry venture was all but devastating to my young ministry mind. I remember laying wide-awake that night while almost every other student was out "in the field" witnessing and selling their books. It was that night that birthed in me this competitive spirit in ministry and the constant feeling that I am either inadequate or I'm not doing enough. So, there I was walking the streets, going door to door, just Jesus and I hoping to make my goal for the day. Although we were selling Christian books, I had to remind myself many times that this was also about ministry and not about earning the most money.

This concept creeps into other areas of church life, ministry efforts, and pastoral assignments as we are constantly tempted to forget the purpose of the work. The loneliness of the toil in ministry is usually the very thing that drives you back to Christ. And that hot afternoon knocking on countless doors alone for 8 hours with one break, I learned to either find Jesus or go crazy. I always reflect back on this experience as a time when I truly felt His presence. But it was not easy since I am very cynical, and often get in the way of heavens communication by thinking too much (I have since learned that prayer can be transferring our random thoughts to heaven). I remember the struggle to believe that He was really walking with me, the battle to press on amidst the slamming doors, and desperately trying to find purpose in this tedious work. Not to mention, the pure anger I felt when it seemed Jesus was nowhere to be found in the most needed time of my life.

I always say this was the best and worst summer of my life. Finding Jesus was the best, but the process was grueling. I am not sure I can exactly remember how I felt but it's etched in my mind as one of those Jacob/Jonah/Joshua experiences all meshed into one. A time of wrestling, running, and reliance where you are holding on for dear life unsure of heavens next move, or your own for that matter.

I continued to move forward, placing one foot in front of the other and at times it felt mechanical, knocking on doors and reciting my speech. *Hello, my name is Joshua and I'm a student working my way through school...* That speech that I repeated so many times, that even today, some 14 years later I could recite it word for word under duress. Okay I digress. In the midst of my spiritual turmoil I turned the corner "following my curb" (colporteur lingo) and arrived on the block that unbeknownst to me, would change my ministry outlook forever.

I walked up to the first house, being mindful of the style of the house, decorations in the window, the toys in the driveway, the flag mounted on the garage. All these subtle things would determine which book I pulled out first. I said my routine silent prayer, wiped the sweat from my upper lip, pulled out my book and with a deep breath approached the door. Ringing twice, knocking three times, waiting, then repeating. An annoying sequence I know, but we were expected to be persistent. A persistence that paid off many times but also resulted in very unhappy neighbors. That was the mystery and the pure dread of ministry, the fact that you have no idea how the person will respond to your efforts. You can have the best intentions and be pouring your heart and effort out and people choose not to respond. That is the beauty and fear of the gospel we share, that people have the choice to accept or decline. The ministers job however is to connect as closely as possible to the Holy Spirit to present the gospel in its very best package as to appeal to the particular soul you encounter. Do you know how hard that is?! By the time you have knocked on 200 doors in a distrustful era, filled with people who do not like home visits and do not want some kid asking them about their spiritual life, you begin to see the next ministry opportunity as a job and not a vocation.

Many of us know how impersonal and how mechanical some of our tasks in ministry can become. We focus too much on obstacles instead of the opportunity to reach this particular person at this particular time for such a time as this. Thankfully while at the door one obstacle had been removed as the front door was already open and only the screen door stood between myself and this unsuspecting family. I could hear them stirring in the living room and squinted my eyes to see through the meshed screen door. I shouted out to let them know I was still there then all of a sudden, I heard a man shout back to me. "Get out, hurry, run, save yourself!", the man blared. At that moment my eyes finally focused on something through the dark screen and to my horror I saw the greatest fear of any door-to-door salesmen. A huge lion-like, chow dog was running in full sprint towards the screen door which I now noticed was slightly ajar. Without a second thought I did a perfect about-face, that would make any Master Guide proud, then ran towards the small gate surrounding their yard.

The chow had burst through the door and I felt his breath as he snapped at my heels. I swung my book back between the dog and I using a textbook maneuver from colporteur dog defense 101. The dog did not seem fazed as I leapt over the gate just as its owner dove for the dog's mane. Although I was out of immediate danger I continued with a brisk jog away from the gate just in case. I gave a halfhearted wave to the owner and did not bother to even toss him one of my free books I usually left at every door. I gathered my things and held my chest to make sure my heart didn't fly out. I survived and was thankfully in one piece.

As hilarious as this experience is to me today, at the time it was a very sobering spiritual experience. It reminded me that I was relying on my own strength. It showed me just how fragile I was in the midst of fear and trouble. It became an example of how I was beginning to view ministry, just run away. This experience stands in my mind as a lesson on perseverance and my innate reaction during conflict. That dog running towards me would foreshadow every tough experience, every difficult member, every unanswered desire, every plan I ever would have that did not go the way I wanted. And the big question that God asked of me is "will you yet again 'get out, hurry, run, save yourself?' Or will you stand firm and know that I am with you?"

A Lion in a Pit on a Snowy Day

Over the years of ministry, I have had to answer God's question about my trust in Him and my fear of obstacles over and over again. It is often easy to want to run up out of the trench because there is a lion (or a dog) at the bottom. But that is why I love the story of Benaiah. In the biblical account it seems this brother has a death wish. We do not know too much about him, but what we do know is that he was basically a Bible super hero. I can imagine young boys whining for the latest Benaiah action figure or sleeping in their favorite Benaiah shorts. I can see little girls with Benaiah posters on their walls and probably being used as side-kicks in their brother's imaginary game of Benaiah versus the lion.

By the time Ben shows up to this pit, with a lion in it, on a snowy day, he has already earned a reputation for killing "lion like men" and is known as a valiant man. So many questions flood my mind, like, why was it snowing? Was it a manmade pit to catch a lion? Was the lion hunting or was Benaiah hunting? How did he kill the lion? Oh, and mostly because of my cynicism who can co-sign on this heroic story since it was a snowy day who could really see this happen? Okay sorry I believe you Benaiah, I do, mostly because I have begun to learn that God can do amazing things through people who jump into pits instead of run away from them. They may be afraid at first but when they make that leap of faith, that fear is replaced with power and a sound thought.

Somehow this man felt it necessary to jump into the trench and kill this lion. I mean think about it, the lion is in a pit, who is he bothering? In my mind Ben does not have to jump but He does. It would be much easier to run away but instead he jumps. He leaps into the fray instead of running away. And for years I have asked myself "why?" Why did you do it Benaiah ? Why run head-on into known danger when you can walk away and save yourself? Why do we run towards ministry knowing its fears, knowing the feelings of unrest, knowing we are inadequate, and not knowing if we are doing enough? Why do Christians, worship leaders, bible workers, evangelists, Sunday school or Sabbath school teachers, Pastors, and lay leaders, why do we run towards this trench called ministry? Why does Ben run towards the pit? I still am not sure I have a good answer, but the best I can come up with is, *compassion*. Yes, maybe with such a valiant story you did not expect that to be the reasoning behind a hardened war hero like Benaiah, but I think "compassion" sums it up. Let me explain.

Maybe Benaiah walked past that pit and heard that lion angrily roaring inside. Maybe he barely heard the roar over the loud gust of wind and snow swirling around. He could have easily ignored it and kept on walking but instead he stops and looks into the pit. Sure enough he sees this lion trapped in this pitted trench unable to get out. The lion would probably eventually die over time with no food and no one to pull him out. And no one would dare try, since this lion had been such a nuisance roaring around searching for anything or anyone to devour. So now in the trench, he is literally no threat to anyone anymore. Anyone except for some weary traveler drudging behind Benaiah through the snow on that same path. It would just be that travelers luck to trip into a huge hole, in the snow, while it is snowing, with no way to exit and then in sheer terror realize your cell mate is a lion. Or maybe the snow was building up and he feared the lion could find a way out and continue terrorizing the towns people. Or maybe it was simple, justice for all the pain the lion had caused. Again, I am just speculating, but maybe Ben jumped in because he could not let anyone fall in. He felt it was his duty, his calling, to jump into the trench and face down this roaring lion before others would. I cannot help but see the spiritual link to Jesus Christ.

Christ chooses from the foundation of the world to jump into this pit and destroy Satan who Peter calls a roaring lion (1 Peter 5:8). Jesus knew that if He did not take that leap to save, people would fall headfirst into sin. Where Jesus sought to save, the devil would make sure to devour. So out of pure compassion and love Jesus jumps into our pit with the lion on a snowy day.

When we follow Jesus into ministry, we are also following Him into trenches and pits to face troubles, in hopes to save others. We do it because He did it for us and because we cannot imagine others not having the same hope we have. Jesus calls us to jump in with Him and trust that He will use us to do more than we thought was humanly possible. I have been used by God in many situations where I know that it was only because of superhuman power that I was still standing. I believe that God can use anyone, we just have to be willing to be used. In the end we can look back and realize that the power of God was in us to do some amazing things for Him. And honestly whether people respond or not, the feeling of Christ in you doing His work, is a priceless feeling. Never let the devil make you think that you do not have power. God can and will use you. The fact that you are reading this book means you are willing to be used. God is with you in the trench and wants to turn you into a lion slayer. Like He said to Joshua, *"Have I not commanded you? Be strong and of good courage; do not be afraid, nor be dismayed, for the Lord your God is with you wherever you go"* (Joshua 1:9).

When I feel discouraged about ministry I will sometimes think back to that day with the dog. I remember that God has given me the power to turn around on my heels, stare the depression, the fear, the anger in the face and say, "Hello my name is Joshua, I am...a minister in the trenches."

The gospel ministry carries many challenges and produces many fears. Here are some of the greatest fears, statements, and questions I have heard stated regarding ministry work.

1. *I am not reaching enough people.* This is the temptation to think that you are never doing enough. It can lead to burn-out and depression because you never know when enough has been done. Read and remember the words in Luke 15:7.

2. *I am not adequate to accomplish the task.* This happens often when we get overwhelmed or begin to compare our work with what others have done. We question if God has given us enough gifts to even complete the work at hand. My prayer for us are in the words in Hebrews 13:20, 21.

3. *Someone else is better than I am.* Again, we start to compare ourselves with others and see the grass as greener on the other side. We measure what we have done and do not consider that each has a totally different situation and journey. Reflect on what Jesus said to Peter in John 21:22.

4. *They will not respond.* The devil often sows this line of doubt into our minds as we focus too much on the negative responses we have had over the years of trying ministry. Let Jesus remind you who people respond to in John 10:27-28.

5. *What will they think or say about me?* We often become self-conscious and turn inward, thinking more about ourselves than the danger of not doing ministry for that individual or people. Let go of your fear and read Jeremiah 1:8, Ezekiel 2:6 for strength.

6. *Have I done enough?* We ask this question because there are no parameters to ministry. It always seems like we can do more. Run to Jesus and know He approves, reflect on Psalm 61:2 and Colossians 3:23-24.

7. *Will I be saved.* We are so used to doing ministry that we find it hard to respond to ministry. We wonder if we are just playing a part in a play or if we can actually benefit from what we are presenting. A temptation that lets you preach to others, but makes you think you are somehow above the message. You unknowingly start to behave like you are the giver of the gospel instead of the proclaimer. Have confidence in your salvation by reading Philippians 1:6 and 2 Timothy 2:13.

A Passion for Souls

Before I went into the ministry my mother asked me a question that still haunts me each day of my ministry. She asked, "Joshua, do you have a passion for souls?" This question has challenged me to connect with God's passion for the people He has called me to reach. I consider Jesus and how He came and showed unconditional love to reach the lost.

I challenge you to ignore the negative and jump in. Develop a passion for souls. In fact, they are the reason you are in ministry. Their presence defines the reason we call it trench ministry. We must realize that we do ministry because of our compassion for others and love for Jesus. This gives us drive, purpose, and passion for our ministry, but it still may not drive away all of our fears. Ministry is also about how God is saving you and turning you into His hero.

One thing I have started to do is to journal and keep a record of the trials and triumphs of ministry. When things get discouraging I can read back and see the journey that God has had me on. Try this and you will be more than surprised when you see things that you had forgotten. Take time to look up the verses that match up with the above 7 fears. Take some time and begin to internalize them for your ministry life. Add your own verses that personally speak to you to the list above and allow the Spirit to lead you. Write out your thoughts and feelings of how God is calming those fears. Remember above all else, God has given us power from the Holy Spirit to do this thing called ministry (Acts 1:8).

#TrenchChronicles

Bang. I jolted awake as the large truck drove over a hole in the road. Each pothole the driver hit made it seem like the entire truck would split in half. Startled, but trying to play off my accidental siesta, I tried to casually stretch and smoothly wiped the small formation of drool developing in the corner of my mouth. I glanced first at the side-view mirror to make sure my car was still securely and safely on the flatbed behind us. Then with a casual glance at the driver, just to make sure he was not sleeping also, I looked back towards the road trying to stay awake. The noise from the windows, the loud diesel engine, and the dull hum of the static radio in the background created the perfect white noise. God knows I was tired, not to mention hot and frustrated from the recent days' experience.

My wife and three-month old daughter and I were about 90 miles from home when the car started overheating. With my car having 250k plus miles there was no telling exactly what was causing this problem. It was a sweltering 100-degree South Carolina humid day at high noon. Probably the worst situation for a small infant and tired mother. My natural instinct was to cuss and scream, but instead God forced a prayer into my spirit. With my track record, my wife waited for the fuse to blow my ticking time bomb, but I stayed calm.

God worked everything out so perfectly, it was scary. In no time, wife and baby were in a friend's car and heading down the highway home as I stayed back to get the car towed. And here I was, riding in the tow truck, fighting sleep and frustration. I should have been counting my blessings and praising God for the miracle He performed, but instead I was griping. So many questions for God. Why did this have to happen? Why is my day such a waste? Why did this have to happen on Father's Day and my first Father's Day at that? Why did our plans have to get ruined? What is wrong with my car? Is it going to cost a lot of money to fix? Should we get a new car? Which car should we get? Can we afford it? "SHUT UP," came the unexpected word from heaven, and only the way God knows how to do. He rebuked me and shifted my focus to the driver sitting next to me. Yes, I had a trial that was happening in my life, but I was still a minister. In the trenches maybe, but I was still a minister with a mission. So, I started to pray for the large fellow next to me drinking energy drinks and eating peanut M&M's. I did not know what to say to witness to this tow truck driver. I remembered I had mentioned earlier that I was a Seventh-day Adventist Pastor. I did not want to be too forward, so I prayed for God to give me an opening. Now the ride had purpose, it had meaning because I left myself and my woes and began to refocus my attention on someone else. And in my intercession the Holy Spirit got excited and found room to work.

With about thirty minutes left in our trip, the large man shouted over the noise of the truck and wind, “excuse me sir, could you tell me about your faith?” That was all a minister needed to hear, music to my ears and for the next thirty minutes we talked about religion, the Bible, the church, and God’s love. I may never know what part that conversation had in the journey God has for that truck driver, but I know that God used me for that moment. It may have even been more for me than for the man, but I know that if I had not put aside my anger toward the trench for a while I would have never noticed the man in the trench right next to me.

Jump

Sometimes the lion is your fear to activate the power and strength God has given us to defeat the enemy’s strongholds in people’s life. Believe it or not, we have access to some real power that can do some real damage in the devil’s kingdom. Let’s not be afraid to jump into the trench and defeat the enemy. As you read this, God is preparing situations for you to be victorious in. We have to be aware of these things and not be afraid of the lions.

▪ Something to Try ▪

Intentionally operate out of your comfort zone and ask God to change your perspective. Ask God to fill you with His Spirit and to refocus and use your fear. Pray that God would give you a burden and passion for souls. Learn to expect and enjoy the Spirit and see what God teaches you about His power and His plan for your life and others.

Reason #6 not to quit ministry:

You've got access to power, therefore, victory is inevitable.

Chapter 7: Dig or Die

When our back is against the wall we discover the kind of person God has called.

2 Kings 3:16-19, MSG
"He then said, "God's word: Dig ditches all over this valley. Here's what will happen—you won't hear the wind, you won't see the rain, but this valley is going to fill up with water and your army and your animals will drink their fill. This is easy for God to do; He will also hand over Moab to you. You will ravage the country: Knock out its fortifications, level the key villages, clear-cut the orchards, clog the springs, and litter the cultivated fields with stones."

■■■

Someone said faith is taking a leap into the darkness. Faith is also realizing that the light shines best in the darkness. Another huge reason trench ministry can be so difficult is because we are in no control over the outcome. We are living between the known and unknown. I have known people who have sold houses, moved to foreign countries, made major investments all in the name of advancing the work for ministry. I have always admired such faith and secretly envied missionaries who can go to the ends of the earth for their faith in Jesus and their passion in His gospel. For many of us our faith is not that great just yet. God has placed us in a small corner of the vineyard and has asked us to grow where we are planted. Can we thrive until He transplants us? Too many times we want to move on to the next big thing without fulfilling God's plan where we are. This is why I love this next story. It involves three armies who are stuck in the wilderness about to die until God gives them a strange job in order for them to stay alive.

The kings from Edom, Israel, and Judah had formed an alliance to defeat Moab, however during a suggested detour they found themselves trapped in the dessert with no water. They may have died had it not been for the counsel they sought from the prophet Elisha who just so happened to be nearby. After the prophet summons a musician to play (which is an interesting nuance in the story) the word of the Lord speaks forth. The command is for them to dig ditches in the valley. Of course, I love the Hebrew translation which reveals the word is actually "trenches". They will not see where the water comes from, but the holes will be full of water. And then just to brag, I love that God tells them how simple this miracle is for Him to do.

Okay so let us not miss the situation in the story. The kings are already in the valley, with no water, tired men and animals, and now they are asked to dig? And not only dig but dig apparently in the heat of the scorching dessert sun since cloud cover would suggest a source for rain. And all this while God brags about how this is an easy thing for Him to do. If it is so easy God, could you just provide some Aquafina bottles to appear on the scene? Okay maybe that's too extreme, but why not just have them wake up to a well already built? You know one of those Jacob or Moses travelling experiences. But this is not what happens in the story. Instead, these tired, thirsty Kings have to decide if they will trust God, suck it up, and dig like God has commanded. They could question His methods all day long but at the moment they had to dig or die.

In ministry we often find ourselves in the valley with a shovel in our hands looking down at the rock-solid ground deciding whether to dig or die. And for us death would mean turning our backs on ministry and giving up on the unknown plans God claims He has for us in our work. I believe you would agree that often times faith in God's word seems easier said than done? It is a nice idea and it makes sense to dig trenches to collect water, but it becomes a little tougher to actually begin digging the ditches. And especially when I am already tired in the valley under the shadow of death. Then we must factor in the fact that there is literally no physical or scientific evidence that what God says is even possible. How do we know for sure that God is going to do it? What if after digging all these trenches He decides to wait just a few more days?

In ministry experience there comes a time when we are in that valley of desperation. This valley may be a location God has asked you to minister. Or with people whom you do not get along. Or to do some task that requires too much of your time or resources. Or He asks you to hold off on your dreams, but you see Him fulfilling your colleagues and friend's dreams. Or you are simply burnt out from exerting so much energy for the work and seeing very little results. These valleys can seem hopeless. Especially in situations where others are flourishing in their ministries and you are stuck to struggle and wait. It is so difficult to wait and be patient, and many times jealousy creeps in. It is hard not to compare yourself with other ministers, especially when you know some are not living a Godly lifestyle, yet they still seem to be blessed. Sometimes it feels like God forces us into the trenches. And let us be honest, if you are like me, you too have given God your share of frustration on these types of arrangements.

In the story it was the King of Edom who suggested they travel a round-about route which led to their dire situation. I can imagine they were pretty upset with him and had their "whoa is us" moments. I am almost sure they asked why this had to happen to them and even regretted starting their quest in the first place. Who knows maybe the quest that you and I are on was not God ordained. Sometimes we dig our own trenches that were never God's design, and we sabotage ourselves. Praise God that He has a plan for our unplanned detours.

In the story, God foresaw their troubles and positions them

near the location of the prophet Elisha for them to seek counsel. God will find a way to show up in our valley moments and give us a word in due season. We must be willing to seek Him in our darkest moments and hold on to the faith that God can still bring us through. Remember that He is always watching and ready to step in when we call out to Him.

So, you are in the valley feeling discouraged, desperately needing direction, remember that Jesus is in the nearby mountain. There is a way out, but we must make the choice to reach out to Him. And here then lies the difficult part because we already know this step. As ministers we have told this to others, we know that God is the source of our strength and that we can always run to Him. That part is easy for us, the difficult part is accepting His time table, or in this story accepting His command to dig trenches. Whether God answers immediately or makes us wait, whether He directs or is vague, if He is loud or silent, there comes a point where our faith is measured. Are we able to exist in the void and trust that He will see us through? The message in this story is not just to exist but to work.

When you are in the trenches of ministry and you question your call, or wonder what God is doing, or do not see any results, or are struggling with sin, or just tired of ministry, the word is to dig. Keep on doing ministry. Sounds hard doesn't it? More than just sounds, it is very hard. I have been there where I just wake up and wonder what and why I am doing what I am doing. I have had those moments when tears come to my eyes and I literally weep wondering where God is taking me. For me I have these moments because I lose sight of my purpose. I forget the reason I am in this thing in the first place. I am in ministry because I followed a call, a move of God on my life that said I would do whatever and go wherever He asked. So, if that includes digging trenches, then my question is how many and how deep?

The hardest thing about trench digging is that it forces you to go deeper into the trench. In other words, it gets harder before it feels easier. When you dig in and go back to work it will be tough to keep your resolve. But like the three kings with their soldiers and animals in the dessert, what choice do we have? When our backs are against the wall, Christ is the only one to call. We learn if we are truly God's men and women. We must spiritually dig in or we will spiritually die.

Prepare for Rain

This also reminds us that the more you dig the better prepared you are for the blessing. The measure of our faith will prepare us to receive more of God's blessings. Let us be clear that you are not working for your blessing, you are preparing. I truly believe that God is constantly and desperately wanting to pour out windows of blessings upon us but we are just not ready. We complain and whine instead of learning from the trial. Every moment God is teaching us, preparing us, holding us. It can seem like He has forgotten us or that the wait is too painful, but this is all a part of His plan.

Our reaction during the wait produces our character and resolve in the triumph. We may think that the wait is too long, and that God should act right away, but it is in His grace that He tarries. For if the rains were to come today we would not be ready to receive it. The rain could have come that very moment, but the men would have drunk for a day and still thirst for the remainder of the journey. If we change our perspective, we can sometimes see the wisdom of God. He can see everything, and we are only looking through a tiny hole compared to his vantage point. This is why we should never complain when we face obstacles.

I know people who get so bent out of shape every time something does not go their way, or when there is a snag in their plans. Wait, that is how I am too. Let us be honest and admit this is a pretty natural human reaction. But we must train ourselves to see opportunities instead of obstacles. Every obstacle is simply an opportunity for God to work His power in us to exercise our patience. He must work in us kingdom characteristics of patience, endurance, and faith. We learn faith through each experience and it reminds us that God is in control. The obstacle gives us time to wait on God. It gives us time to prepare for His miracle. And most importantly it makes room for His glory.

The task at hand may seem daunting. It may seem like busy work, but it is preparing you. The more we prepare, the more we can receive. The more I educate myself the more prepared I can be for a job that comes my way. What if I just said, "God I want that job, why are you not giving it to me?" Instead, ask God for the job and go prepare for the skills you will need to receive the job. In this, God reminds us that we often don't dig enough because we don't think He is big enough. The reason you don't receive the blessings you could have is because you spent too much time in the trench complaining instead of in the trench digging.

Prep Work

This story also speaks to us about preparation. God wants to get us involved. It can seem as if God is working in reverse when we are in the trench. I found that He does this to teach us to prepare. If we truly believe He will bring the rain, we will prepare the trench. Like Elijah on mount Carmel we will dig the trench before we see the fire. He wants us to rely on His word instead of on our worries. In relying on Him we get closer to Him and receive more peace. So, this is what He does. He has us build the boat before we see the flood. He has us build the alter before we have a sacrifice. He has us cast the net before we see the fish. Look, he could send the flood and then tell us to build the boat but then we would say we had no time to prepare. He could send the rain before the trenches but then we would have to dig muddy holes in the rain. We must learn to trust God's foresight and learn to prepare for the blessings already in store for us. We must sit in the trench and dig some ditches. So, the question becomes, "How great is your faith?" How much do you believe that He is going to open up the windows of heaven upon you?

If He wants to send you to that larger church assignment, then are you reading, studying, praying so that when it comes you will be ready? If He has a million-dollar donor ready to pour into your project, do you have a plan to manage those funds? If He wants to double those coming to your community center, do you have the space to hold and organizational skills to manage them? Are you digging? We often want the blessings but are not prepared to receive them. Instead of focusing on what God is, or is not doing fast enough, focus on what God is asking you to prepare for, what He is doing. Basically, start digging trenches, which translates into exercise your faith through work. If you could see past your hurt, your pain, your thirst, your self-pity, you would see how vital it is that you dig. There is so much more that God wants to do but we hinder God because of our lack of faith. Our lack of faith comes from our cynicism and analysis of what we think is possible and how we feel. God wants to get us to a place where we do not trust our feelings, we just trust His word.

I often admire children or even those who claim not to have prestigious education. Their faith is often untethered and free to believe without the hindrance of facts or feelings. They have learned that no matter the situation, God is still the best thing going. Who else are they going to turn to and what else are they going to trust? We must learn that we cannot think or plan our way out of life's deepest valleys. The only way out is with a shovel called faith. When you are in the valley, deep in the trench of despair, please do not give up. Grab the shovel and dig in deeper. And like one of my elders said about his experience digging ditches, "eventually you will find water if you dig deep enough, it's just a fact".

Trusting in God will never fail us, it may not come immediately, but the wait is the preparation for the blessing. It is your choice right now. You are standing in the place He has ordained with the tools He has given. What will you do? How long will you last? Will you dig in? It is time to Dig or Die.

#TrenchChronicles

My arms felt like noodles, I could barely turn the steering wheel of my 2006 Altima as I backed out of the CrossFit gym parking lot. I made it to the stop sign, looked to the left for traffic and saw the hospital in the distance out of the corner of my eye. As traffic cleared, I made the right turn, thinking about how in just a few months that hospital would play a major part in my life. My wife was seven months pregnant, a mighty miracle considering we had already experienced two miscarriages. The first miscarriage had occurred at 6 months and resulted in a still birth, a traumatic experience we feared could be repeated.

These months of pregnancy had required us to dig into our

faith reserves and put what we learned about God to the test yet again. As I crossed through the last intersection before the street that led home, I said a short prayer. "Lord, please give us a beautiful baby, an alive baby, an intelligent baby, and a normal baby." The last prayer for a normal baby was of deep concern as through our time being pregnant we had been scared with possible spina bifida and down syndrome. My wife was starting to have some of the same symptoms as last time that lead to the demise of Kiaya. We had been back and forth to specialists, routine visits to our OBGYN, and now my wife was on bed rest. Things were stable and we were digging in to see what God would do.

As I parked the car I went up the stairs exhausted from the workout but excited to see Kim and her baby bump. It was about midday, I had taken the day off as my wife and I sat together relaxing. Then suddenly, Ring! Ring! My heart skipped as we saw the hospital number come up on her cellphone screen. So far, these calls had come and been routine calls, false alarms, or regular updates. No matter how good the probability had been, each time we feared they were calling because something was wrong. This time, we were correct. As the conversation ended we scrambled into high gear as the medical professionals alerted us that they had missed something and my wife, Kimberly needed to be admitted immediately. This was worst case scenario and a cause for serious alarm.

Kim was admitted and the doctor examined her and told us the baby had to come out. We sat bewildered with mixed emotions. On one hand my wife was tired with being pregnant, she had gone through so much and her blood pressure was so high. On the other hand, we wanted our child to be safe and not have to stay in the NICU. It was time to dig into the trench, hold on to the God we had met during the two-prior crisis. Unable to bear the idea that we could face three miscarriages being this close to a successful birth, I turned my head and looked for God. Where was He?

The medicine was given and the contractions began. One of the worst things in life is to see the one you love in pain and be literally helpless to give relief. Hours passed. Pain increased. Prayers were repeated. I looked for God in the trench.

Where was He?

The evening and the morning meshed into one as the doctor finally came into the room. She said it was time to deliver. Easy for her to say now that she had a good night's rest during the most agonizing time of our life. I watched as she literally put her entire hand into my wife, felt around then used an instrument to puncture and release her water. My wife clenched and grunted in pure agony. I looked away, trying to find the Healer.

Where was He?

Beep! Beeeeep! Beep! The cadence and tone of the beeps triggered my inner panic button. This meant something was terribly wrong. The baby's heart rate had dropped significantly and she was losing oxygen. The expression on the face of the doctor changed from the casual "everything will be alright, I do this all the time", to a face that said, "nurses, this is not a drill, we may lose this baby." And as if a switch was flicked, the two nurses and doctor turned to four nurses, as the doctor rushed to prep for an emergency C-section and the nurses prepped my wife for surgery. I watched, impressed and scared to death as each nurse methodically played their role. Within a few minutes my wife was out of the room off to surgery. A nurse told me it would be ok and handed me some scrubs. She left to allow me to put them on. I did, then sat there stunned, dazed, disoriented. I thought I heard something, I looked and there was nothing.

Where was He?

Then I heard it. I looked down by my right and saw my scripture cards I kept with me. I lifted the first card and began to read Isaiah 30:19, *"For the people shall dwell in Zion at Jerusalem: You shall weep no more. He will be very gracious to you at the sound of your cry, when He hears it. He will answer you."* And I began to weep. I fought it back as the nurse came in and then lead me to where the surgery would take place. The doctor came out and assured me all would be well but nothing on her face would let me believe her. Because of the nature of the operation I was unable to be in the room. I watched as at least eight different people moved into the room with my wife and unborn daughter.

I could see Kim but I couldn't touch her. I wanted to run to her and hold her and say I was there and God would deliver our baby. But I couldn't do that. I had no idea what God would allow to happen. The only thing I knew was that He was at least aware of our situation. I had heard His voice but I needed to see Him.

Where was He?

The door closed and it seemed time stopped. I was in the void. No nurse was there in the hall. I could hear nothing except for an occasional beeping sound. Even my cell signal was cut off and the frequent texts to my mother ceased. I was alone. My wife was alone, unconscious in her dreamlike thoughts as they cut and pulled on her body. My baby was...I couldn't finish that thought. I did not want to attach myself to her just yet. Then I felt it.

A warm feeling came over my entire body, I looked to my right and I saw Him. No, not like an actual figure but I saw His presence. It is hard to put into words but He turned and looked at the door and just smiled. Nothing was said. I turned also and stared at the door. We dug in. Then I heard Kaleah – *the voice of God* – cry from beyond the door. The door opened. She was beautiful. She was normal. She was intelligent. She was alive.

In that moment He reminded me that He had been there through it all. Through the loss of my first child, through the pain, through the fear, through the anger...He had always been there...with me...in the trench.

It's Pouring

He says He wants to open the windows of heaven to us. Showers of blessings is what the song says. I have discovered that there is really no place else to turn but to Him. His presence is always pouring over us in ways we never would expect. In times of trial you have a choice to make, I choose Him every time. Try learning from the trials and begin to see obstacles as opportunities. Take some time and think about the areas in your life where God wants you to dig in and trust in Him. Now stop looking for the rain and look for Him. He is the water; He is your blessing, He is life.

▪ Something to Try ▪

We keep a prayer and praise jar where we drop notes with those times when it was tough to trust in God. Looking back allows you to see how God was working all along.

Reason #7 not to quit ministry:

There is so much more if you can just dig in and trust Him

Chapter 8: Record! Write! Run!

When He gives the vision, we must respond.

Habakkuk 2:2 NASB
"Then the LORD answered me and said, "Record the vision And inscribe it on tablets, that the one who reads it may run."

Leadership

Undoubtedly, when engaging in any form of ministry you will be working with other people who also want to do ministry. And when there are different ideas on how to accomplish this feat there can be difficulties. Especially if you have been assigned as the leader over a set group of people, you may face various nuances regarding your style of leadership. The biggest obstacle for me has been learning how to "lead people" versus "taking people". In many cases you will have a direction or vision that you want to take the people in, but you are the only one who shares this conviction. The question rises as to how you can lead people somewhere they do not wish to go?

Many would say that you are not a leader until you have

followers. So now you develop the urge to convince or manipulate people to agree or at least go along with you. However, problems usually arise when people catch on that you are trying to change their minds. They may fight back and make things harder. This leads to a strange game of politics that creeps into the ministry as people fight to get their own way. And as the designated leader, it is extremely hard to relinquish control, especially your conviction on where the ministry needs to go.

In many cases I felt so strongly that some decision or direction was correct that I could not imagine considering any other path. It becomes extremely difficult to "let it go" when you strongly believe you are correct. Depending on your personality you may not feel a need to exert your opinion above others, however, the dichotomy of emotions remains a frustration. Angst in knowing the vision may never be realized is another cause for ministry burnout or wanting to leave ministry all together.

It is often easy for me to observe businesses and organizations and see more unity and cooperation than in ministry. When you are dealing with volunteers or elected officers, you have little control over your team. Even with the teams you may have handpicked there remains difficulties in fostering motivation and commitment. This adds a whole different dynamic to how you interact. There will undoubtedly be some things you will not say that needs saying, but feel it may offend your volunteer. With no hiring and firing power you are at the mercy of the whims and desires of those in your ministry. Not to mention the outside demands of school, careers, families, traveling, and just the various demands of life that challenge the time of most church volunteers. At times it seems everything is pulling people away from ministry. If not careful, it is easy for people to put ministry on the back burners.

This arises because people do not understand how our relationship should be with ministry. It is not my life and my ministry, it is my life of ministry. Everything we do, no matter how mundane, should center us back to our ministry. Now to be fair there are many people who take ministry in their lives very seriously. Some take it too seriously. But at the end of the day you are interacting with all sorts of different personalities, worldviews, and opinions. It can be extremely hard to lead a ministry in any direction, even if everyone says they are following Christ.

One important truth to remember is that principles are forever, but practices are always changing. Developing a set of principles or standards that the ministry can agree upon is a great first start. Once you can differentiate between the two it helps clarify the areas where people actually agree. Most people argue about practices, where they agree on principles. The way I have learned to do this is by doing a "core value evaluation". Basically, a simple test that asks questions as to what your group values. It may be that the group values social justice, education, and children. This becomes the start to the focus and the passion that will drive the ministry. As a leader you cannot lead people unless you know how they think and what they think. Even if 'what they think' is not what you hoped, you now can unpack 'why they think' the way they do. And when you understand 'why they think' it, you will more easily be able to lead them towards change.

This albeit is a long grueling process that may seem pointless, but it pays off in the end. Depending on the group and education level these steps may take longer. Some people are just not used to filling out evaluations or giving good feedback on paper. In my particular assignment or my ministry department, I have had to adjust my communication style according to the level of my volunteers. Being that I am usually considered an outsider, there are cultural ways of getting information from them that I had to admit I did not understand. I had to identify a co-laborer that did understand the culture and could communicate to them. Once I found this person, my work became easier. My job now was simply to communicate to him and he translated to the others. Even though it went against my ego I found that this was what needed to be done if I wanted to make progress, I had to delegate and trust the process.

You must learn to study your people. They communicate, you just have to learn how they communicate. I remember when my wife, who is an introvert, and myself, an extravert, started dating. During times of conflict or misunderstanding I had to find different ways to communicate with her. Passing notes, texting, giving her space, and avoiding raising my voice were all ways that aided in our relationship. However, with previous relationships some of these tactics failed to work. Understanding the communication language of your volunteers can be difficult. As stated earlier, if you learn to communicate to your executive team they will often times know how best to communicate to the others.

When interacting in ministry, you are meshing yourself with people to create the body of Christ. In order to truly be in unity, you must learn the people to whom you are ministering. This does not mean you have to be best friends, but it means you have to come together for a common goal. And you need to be confident that everyone can clearly see that we are here for the same purpose. So, establishing that purpose by understanding the core values is crucial. Remember that as a group the "core values evaluation" is not a decision on the core values, but rather a discovery. There is no right, or wrong answer and it should simply reveal what or how the group feels.

Once you understand core values you can then move to a clear purpose or position statement. This will answer the question; "Why do they need us?". This needs to be made extremely clear in everyone's mind. Many groups, especially if extremely conservative, will directly opt to copy and paste Matthew 28:29-30 to be their purpose/position statement. You have to teach and explain that there needs to be a more specific and heart wrenching purpose/position that speaks to that particular group's core values. Once a group begins to grasp their purpose, this must be repeated each time they come together. In a church I suggest making it apart of your morning litany during weekly worship.

At some point, possibly after the purpose or prior to, the group needs to answer the question regarding God's vision. Allow the group to break into small teams and with prayer, discuss what they have observed God doing in their community. The purpose and position of the church helps center on the unique value your church has for the community. The vision of God shows you how He will use this group to accomplish His overall goal for the community. In essence, the vision helps you to see, at least a small glimpse, of where God is taking the ministry.

Once the vision is clear it is time to write the vision by deciding on particular goals for the ministry group. There should be short-term goals and long-term goals. Long-term goals should look beyond what is seemingly possible and reach towards the humanly unattainable God-size goal in the distant future. The short-term goals should be detailed, fairly attainable benchmarks for each week or month. These goals should be revisited regularly and evaluated as progress is made.

Once the vision is clear and written, people must now run to actually strategize for implementation. This is not a statement but a document where you figure out the "how" for the goals set forth. This is the "practice" part of the "principles" that often cause so much disagreement. But if you have done your due diligence in the first three areas you should find it easier to come together by this stage. You must understand leadership because while you are leading this process you are not leading the outcome. The Holy Spirit must be allowed to lead and direct the people to the conclusion He gave you. This process allows people to be open to His promptings. Sometimes they will get it wrong but you should wait to intervene. Unless directly asked, I would suggest you observe and facilitate. Operate more as a coach and not a chief. You must realize that your role as a ministry leader is a very delicate role. People must buy into the plan and not be forced into the plan. For me this has meant stagnation many times. Yes, it is extremely frustrating, but you have to allow people to grow and you have to learn to water them. Sometimes we give up on people too easily when all they need is nurturing.

When you can master observation and facilitation you will see so much more progress. I have had churches that moved quickly through this process and we accomplished a lot of ministry in the community. And I have had churches that moved snail-paced through this process and we did not accomplish much in the community. I learned that in the latter group, that the work was seen in their growth as ministers. The process was to reach them for that time whether or not we baptized the entire block may not have been the purpose for that time. However, if I had asserted my authority it would have spoiled all that needed to take place organically in that church.

Remember leaders do not have power simply because of their position. I cannot just assert my positional authority whenever I please and think things will get done. Well I guess things will get done but these things will not last. A ministry is truly successful when the leader leaves and ministry still thrives. In order for this to happen, in order for officers in the church to relinquish the positions they have held for years, we must teach people the ‘why’. This goes into the subject and importance of good discipleship practices. It is easy to get discouraged as a ministry leader, pastor, or minister when you do not understand your own ‘why’ or purpose.

The great commission tells us that we need to make disciples. Our job is to get our ministry group to constantly and consistently follow Jesus in order to get others to follow Jesus. If we think our purpose is to lead people, or accomplish some numerical goal, or to end up in the news then we have greatly cheapened our brand. We are simply placed here to get people to follow Jesus. And that alone is harder than it sounds. Remember that Jesus only had twelve followers. He chose to pour into these twelve people in hopes that they would each pour into someone else and then the ministry grew exponentially. The success was when this actually happened, when apostles like Paul left a church, the church still thrived because they understood their purpose.

Now let us talk about what we started out with in the first place. How do you deal with people who, after all this, still never buy into the ministry, leadership, or the process? What do you do with trouble makers and outliers who have literally been sent by the enemy to disrupt the process? I will give three things that I have tried that have worked for me.

Pray the enemy out.

This is extremely important and should not be skipped past. When you bathe your ministry in prayer you remind everyone who is really in charge. You set a precedence for Christ to move in people's hearts. Every meeting that I chair, I make sure that my devotion and prayer last at least fifteen and in some cases even thirty minutes. People may want to complain but it forces you and them to be subservient to the Spirit. In fact, I am even careful with my language during meetings and after the devotion. I never say, "now it is time for the meeting to begin", I instead say, "now the meeting will continue." I want them to understand that the meeting is prayer, it is devotion. How can we meet about ministry without invoking the spirit of ministry to lead us? When you start to pray specifically for the enemy to leave your presence and for Jesus to remain, one of two things must happen. Either the persons who are being used by the enemy will be moved and released from the power of the enemy, or those very people will leave your company. Either way the Spirit of God must drive out the enemy. And even if these people physically remain in your presence, you will be filled with so much power that you will easily counter any of their oppositions. There have been times where things have been said that should have derailed the group and God shut my mouth or caused certain people not to hear the statement that would have otherwise aggravated them. And I have seen how God has given me superhuman wisdom on the spot to defuse trouble.

Take a personal approach.

Visitation or just being intentional about developing relationships has a huge payout. As much as it can be awkward, being able to interact with someone outside of a meeting is priceless. It causes you to see them as human, and they to see you the same. You want to allow your hearts to attach. Even if you disagree, it will not be a fight because you are now more connected. This step takes time and can be extremely tedious, but if you commit to it, you will see results. I used to think visitation got in the way, but I found it cannot afford to be avoided. Visitation is the ministry and it is one of the best things that advances ministry.

Take Spiritual authority.

There will be times that you have to assert your leadership authority. Whether you pull them aside for a small meeting or are forced to do it in the large meeting, there are times when foolishness cannot go unchecked. You must protect the majority of people from the poison that may be seeping into your ministry. As long as you are filled with the Spirit, you can do this in a way that is loving but assertive. People will respect you for it, and many times, thank you. Sometimes you have bullies who just have never had anyone to put them in check. As the leader it is your job to know how and when to do this. Be decisive and be swift. Make sure you have prayed before-hand and have the word of God as your backing. I have never exerted my spiritual authority in this way until I have spent at least an entire day in prayer and Bible study. You need to be sure that you will not regret your method or decision in the future.

Reason #8 not to quit ministry:

There is a plan, there is a process.

Chapter 9: Split the Hallow

He breaks us but fills us.

Judges 15:18, NASB
"Then he [Sampson] became very thirsty; so he cried out to the Lord and said, "You have given this great deliverance by the hand of Your servant; and now shall I die of thirst and fall into the hand of the uncircumcised? So, God split the hallow place that is in Lehi, and water came out, and he drank; and his spirit returned, and he revived..."

■■■

Sometimes you need God to split the hallow place. There is a point that the busyness of ministry, the work of the church, the caring for the sick, the encouraging words, all leads us to a place of dryness. If we are not careful we will spend all of our energy ministering to others and have nothing left for ourselves. It is easy to feed so much, that we forget to eat. Not only is it vital that we have streams flowing into our spirit, we also need balance in our lives. Burnout is a state of emotions that can lead us to a place where we loathe ministry. A place of dryness where we question if this is what God really wanted from us. We can trick ourselves to think that this is what it means to die to self, that God requires us to be exhausted and stressed. We may think that our duty is to give over everything to the people, even our peace and sanity. However, this is a lie and a device used by the enemy to make us resent the very thing we proclaim.

Paul makes it clear in 1 Corinthians 9 that while there is a duty to be all things to all men, he still had a duty to make sure he was saved. *"But I discipline my body and bring it into subjection, lest, when I have preached to others, I myself should become disqualified." (v. 27)* There is always that sneaky temptation when doing ministry that what you are giving is only for them, not for you. This happens when we only study the Bible for a sermon, lesson study, or just to encourage others. Instead we must pay close attention to the dry areas that are forming in our lives. When we cry out to God in these times, this cry is the best thing we can do. God will show us ways to be filled up again. He will be the water that quenches our spiritual thirst. In fact, as the illustration with Samson suggests, God will split the ground for us and in that trench, fill it with water. Sometimes God creates trenches in our lives to get our attention, so He can fill us.

The life of Christ is the best example of balance in ministry that we can find. He made sure there was time for His father, His family, and His friends. This should be how we think of balance in our lives. In fact, if Jesus had not made time for His father, He would not have been able to give His best. We should never feel guilty for taking time to rest and recuperate. The more connected we are to the father, the better we will be given in ministry. We have power when we are in constant connection to the source. Our desire should be to plug into the father each day so that our light will be continuous. So many times, we do ministry wearing a battery pack instead of a plug. We want to use stored power from weeks ago instead of fresh from the source. We must present to people being connected ourselves. This does not mean we have to always give people what God gave only for us. There will be times I catch myself spending time with God and secretly writing a sermon. I am thinking this would be great for someone else to hear instead of soaking up what God has for me. He wants time for Him to just fill us for us.

When we speak of balance there are three areas that I like to focus on. As mentioned above, these are; father, family, friends.

Father

Make time to let God fill you up. Spend time each day in a devotional study that is simply for your edification. Ask God what He is trying to teach you in the text. Find out how the story or verse relates to your life and situation. Create a prayer wall, or prayer book that you keep just between you and God. Even in marriage, I think it is important for each spouse to have their own secret place with God. (That's about the only secret place you can have in marriage). It is also crucial to have someone who will be like a mentor or minister for you. Find someone you trust who calls you and pours into you, a program you watch, someone that gives you thoughts outside of yourself. Hearing new thoughts is important to create a holistic person. There are some things you will not see simply because of your worldview. God often uses other people to show us Himself in new ways. Sometimes when God shows me a peek of His relationship with another, it makes me jealous that much more for our relationship to be taken to the next level.

Lastly, make sure you enjoy the Sabbath. As a ministry leader it can be tempting to view the Sabbath as a day of work instead of rest. Especially for a pastor, this is the day where we do most of our work. You can begin to dread the Sabbath if you are not intentionally creating balance. To keep the Sabbath a delight here are some ways you may want to try.

Delegate, share the load, do not try to do everything yourself.

1. Schedule each hour and make time for yourself.
2. Study and prepare through the week so that you're not cramming the day before.
3. Keep a specific time for your family that everyone looks forward to on the Sabbath.
4. Schedule the day before as a day off.

Family

While Jesus made many statements about leaving and hating your family, in context you must understand that Jesus spent time and had much love for his family. His first miracle was administered at the request of his mother. Towards the end, His brothers were great supporters of His ministry. He spent time as a boy learning carpentry work from His dad. And even on the cross, He made sure to remember His mother. And in many ways, you could say that the entire people of Israel belong to Him as His children. The famous statement He makes on the hill looking over Jerusalem about desiring to gather them under His wing (Matthew 23:37). He spent most of His ministry speaking directly to Jewish people which can also show a commitment to family first. There is this idea of concentric circles of concern that we learned in college. Of course, there is a book with the same name that is a good read. This principle simply reminds us that we minister to those closest to us first and then move outside the circle. Our families are our first priority in ministry. No matter how busy I am, I have always made time for my family. And for those who are married, it is especially crucial to keep regular date nights with your spouse. You should guard your family time like you guard the sacred Sabbath hours. Whether you pick regular times per day or week, make sure nothing or no one disturbs that time.

Friends

When I think of friends I think of social interaction and fun. So, whether or not you have a core group of friends you hang out with, make time to interact with people on a social level and have fun. In my current assignment, I do not have any friends that live even remotely near, but I still make a point to stay connected. Some of my friends and I started a group chat using iMessage that allows us to have that social interaction from afar. These interactions are crucial to your sanity and will allow you to get encouragement and rejuvenation. You also need to schedule times per day or week that you dedicate to just having fun. Again, Jesus gives us the example as we find Him visiting people's houses for meals, going to weddings, and other social gatherings. It may not be overt in the scriptures, but I believe Jesus knew how to have fun. I mean how can you be at a wedding and not?

Here are the top 5 things I like to do for fun.

1. Read with my wife
2. Play video games
3. Take Vacations
4. Dinner out
5. Exercise

Remembering the three F's of balance hopefully will become a part of your life. There is one last thing I want to share specifically for Pastors. I remember when I first became a Pastor I focused too much on the F's and not enough on my ministry. I spent too much time watching TV, going out with friends, or whatever. I did not have a good schedule or structure to get my ministry tasks done during the week. Wednesday nights and Saturday mornings were the only times I really did anything with ministry. This was partly because I was lazy, but also because I had not been taught what Pastor's did during the week. Some years ago, a good friend of mine and colleague, Pastor Terrance Taylor, introduced to me this weekly schedule called Sowing and Reaping P.O.W.E.R. This program has revolutionized my productivity, my ministry, and my balance. Please take time to read how it works in the appendix.

I believe that I am more ready to do things for others when I have allowed God to do for me. My ministry is a response to His goodness in my life, it is not a job. It is a part of who I am. And the only way I keep my identity is by being intentional. So, before you quit on ministry try incorporating balance into your life. It will keep things in perspective and give you streams of life to thrive on, even in the trench.

Reason #9 not to quit ministry:

In the trench, He knows how to fill us up.

Chapter 10: Between the Mountain and the People

We discover God when we focus on His mission.

Deuteronomy 5:4,5 NASB
"The Lord spoke to you face to face at the mountain from the midst of the fire, while I was standing between the Lord and you at that time, to declare to you the word of the Lord; for you were afraid because of the fire and did not go up the mountain."

Luke 9:37-39 NASB
"On the next day, when they came down from the mountain, a large crowd met Him. And a man from the crowd shouted, saying, "Teacher, I beg You to look at my son, for he is my [v]only boy, and a spirit seizes him, and he suddenly screams, and it throws him into a convulsion with foaming at the mouth; and only with difficulty does it leave him, mauling him as it leaves."

■■■

As disciples, engaged in ministry, we often find ourselves between the mountain and the people. Tasked with the awesome assignment to reveal Christ to the people and to see Christ in the people. We seek to have those mountain transfiguration moments, just not at the expense of forgetting those in the valley overtaken by cosmic forces (Matthew 17). The temptation of course is to remain on the mountain top and believe that only there can we find God. In seclusion, distant from the problems of others, high above and away from the valley. But in our quest for God we found Jesus who showed us that there can be no joy on top of the mountain when souls are dying at the foot, in the valley.

We decided to follow Jesus, pick up our cross slipping and sliding down the rough side of the mountain. So here is where ministry takes us, back into the fire, deeper into the thicket, fighting in the fray. We of course do this simply because Jesus did this when He left His throne in glory. We imitate Him and claim the same mission to "seek and save the lost". For we are disciples, following our master to the death, learning from Him, imitating Him, ministering with Him. And oh yes, in the trenches with Him. And this point must not be forgotten; we are in the trenches because that is where He is.

But in this position, there are two temptations that I often struggle with. The scripture tells us that Jesus took Peter, James, and John with him on the mountain top. This story, as told in Matthew chapter 17 involves the glorification or transfiguration of Jesus. In this moment Moses and Elijah appear on the scene to encourage their Lord. Moses must have found this position ironic for he was often climbing mountains to be engulfed by the glory of God during the Exodus, but now he watches as God Illuminates God.

Jesus stands in the position Moses stood in as intercessor for the people. A sure temptation to stay on the mountain and bask in the glory and leave the sinners to their demise with the demons below. Peter chimes in while seeing and hearing this awesome scene and suggests they build three tabernacles, one for Jesus, Moses, and Elijah. But while Peter's vision may have come from a good place His timing was misplaced. The conclusion of the story tells us how detrimental such a project would have been to those in need in the valley.

This is the first temptation I often fight against, I become so distracted by institution and tradition that I forget the main work of saving those in the valley. It is so easy to get caught up in building tabernacles on the mountain when there are more important things to be done in the valley. For me "the mountain" is my desire for notoriety. You know, that whole "tower of babel syndrome" where we want to make a name for ourselves and leave behind a legacy. It also means focusing too much on institution instead of momentum and movement. And in some cases, my desire to place men on pedestals that rival Jesus Christ. Yet my mind must always go back to discovering what is the main thing. What is my mission? Answering this question always refocuses me to what I am supposed to be doing. Seeking and saving the lost.

Peter is such an easy character to identify with for those dedicated to ministry. I had the pleasure of playing the role of the ex-fisherman turned fisher of men, in an Easter Passion Play at Andrews University where I attended Seminary. The play was a serious production that attracted thousands from near and far to witness the live interactive dramatized extravaganza. This production took place both doors and outdoors as the campus was transformed into a middle eastern region some 2,000 years ago. We were outfitted with appropriate costumes and spent weeks memorizing our lines. I found my lines extremely unsettling since I would focus mainly on emotionally depicting Peter's denial of Christ. We may have rehearsed the scene twenty times at least and over 100 times if we include my own personal mirror rehearsals. I have my over-sentimental moments, just like the rest of us (I'd like to think), but this experience lead to a moment I did not expect. I remember vividly breaking down in my apartment and just weeping uncontrollably. You see I had truly embraced the character. I began to feel like I was Peter, as if I had actually been around that fire and denied Jesus. For years I had read the story and at times felt sorry for Peter and sometimes even anger for his quick ability to deny God. But now in my room, a puddle forming on my comforter where my head lay, I begin to understand why Peter did what he did. The answer was pretty obvious, yet I had never felt it before. I knew why Peter denied Jesus because so often in ministry I had been ready to do the same.

It was fear, plain old fear that gripped Peter and the disciples that fateful passion week. Fear of the Jews, fear of the Romans, fear of death, fear of crucifixion, fear of breaking tradition, etc. It was easier to run, to deny, to quit. All that talk in John 13 from Peter saying he was willing to die for Jesus was a front. And here is my second struggle; and where I often find myself in the trench, afraid to walk down the crucifixion road with my Lord.

Church history tells us Peter did not see himself worthy to die the same way as His Lord. Looking back on his fear is why I believe Peter, finally facing death, asks to be crucified upside down. Peter has been converted and he was ready to follow Jesus all the way, even death on a cross. But many of us are not there yet. Or at least we teeter as to what it means to truly pick up our cross, or as I put it "tackle the beast of ministry". The temptation I often feel is fear which leads me to deny my mission to Christ.

As the verse to one of my favorite hymns says, "prone to wander, Lord, I feel it, prone to leave the God I love". It is the crazy sad irony that brings me to tears that I would walk away from the God that I love. Peter goes away weeping in despair from the crucifixion scene and the weight of his own denial. But later we find Peter running head-on to the empty tomb. Whatever fears we possess, disappointments, depressions, anxieties, apprehensions we harbor, can be left at the cross. The empty tomb is evidence that Jesus is bigger than all of that and His mission is primary. As we are in His will we too will conquer and arise victorious with whatever tasks He commands.

There is a temptation that can keep us from embracing our

task, and it is one I know my fellow ministers often struggle with. This is illustrated in the book of John chapter 21 where Jesus has cooked breakfast for disciples who all but walked away from ministry. Jesus knows Peter feels horrible about denying His Master three times and wants to redeem him. He asks him three times if Peter loves him and gives the charge to then "feed my sheep". In other words, if you love me stop moping around and get back to doing ministry. Jesus even goes as far as to make reference to how Peter would have to die for the ministry of Jesus. This of course flairs up the initial fear Peter had and the reason He may have denied Jesus in the first place. I love verse 20 because this is when the story becomes real. (Probably for me, the realist moment in scripture.)

Peter turns around looks at John, who is eavesdropping so well, he is able to recount the story in his book. Peter then asks Jesus what will happen to John, will John have to die also? In their constant competition Peter is now even concerned with the manner of their deaths or at least in some way comparing their ministries. It is right here I see us ministers, as much as we hate to admit it, we constantly fight against the temptation to compete with our colleagues in ministry. It is too easy to compare ourselves with those who are the same age, education, status and question "why I am not as far as they are?"

I admit that I have found myself measuring my accomplishments, questioning their motives, and even analyzing sermons. Let me be clear, it's not that I hate on those God has called, or that I wish to have a monopoly on success in ministry. No, the reasons center back to my own fears and inadequacies. I wonder if I am really doing all that God wants me to do. I fear that there is more that God has ordained for me that I am not doing. And this leads to wondering if I am even useful at all. There it is; I fear becoming irrelevant in the fight against evil. I am afraid that "doing my part" just isn't good enough. And so, when God asks me if I love Him and tells me I will have to die, it scares me. More so because I do not think that should be my end. I can be of use for you like John, I can do more, use me in a different way. But the answer Jesus gives Peter is the answer He gives us in verse 22. Jesus said to him, *"If I will that he remains till I come, what is that to you? You follow Me" (John 21:22, NKJV).*

When I am tempted to measure myself with others and their success in ministry, or jealous of their seemingly perfect ministry connection to God, I must remember to keep my eyes on Jesus. My task is to seek and save the lost, to travel between the mountain and the people. Interceding, going up and down the mountain reconnecting people with their Savior. Jesus did it for the "joy that was set before Him" and that joy was you and I (Hebrews 12:2). When we connect with that kind of love for those in the valley, we discover renewed reasons for our ministry. We may have some trials but as long as we are following Jesus, we have purpose.

I Like to See People Win

One of my young friends and mentees, Raymond, best taught me the lesson of following Jesus to love. Raymond is diagnosed as Autistic and has trouble with verbal communication but is a very bright young man. He would come over my house and we would play on the Xbox Kinect. His favorite game to play was bowling, he just couldn't get enough of seeing the pins fall down. But what intrigued me was how non-competitive he was while playing. Most boys his age are very selfish and competitive, but not Raymond. Anytime it was my turn to play he would scream and cheer me on shouting, "Get a Strike Pastor Nelson, C'mon, get a strike." Now I can't tell you how much hearing those words motivated and improved my virtual bowling game simply because of the pressure not to let him down. So, when I would get a strike, which was quite often I might add, he would go through the roof with excitement. It got contagious and I in turn started rooting him on to get strikes. Soon we forgot all about the score and just started enjoying seeing all the pins fall down.

Afterwards I wondered why he didn't care that I beat him. It then hit me that Raymond just liked to see people win. At the end of the day no matter what your situation, in whatever trench or unfortunate situation you have been born in, lead to, or fallen in, when it comes to ministry we just like to see people win. I crave this trench called ministry because like Jesus I yearn to save souls, even if it's just one. I keep on following Him because I just like to see people win.

This reality, this following is why I exist. I live to do trench ministry. I thrive in the valley because it is where I find Jesus. There He is, yes, the son of David riding on a colt listening to the shouts and praises, but He is also the thirsty traveler at the well meeting a woman from Samaria. There He is, transfigured on the mountain, but also with no place to lay His head. I see Him ascending into the clouds with a promise to return as King, but He is also in the sanctuary pleading His blood for the least, the last, and the lost. And yes, there He is on the cross winning through dying just so we can live. So, I have learned to live between the mountain and the valley because I am confident that since He won, I have won. And if I have won, I know others can win.

Victory Promised

The night Peter denies Jesus, Matthew 26:75 tells us that "Peter remembered the word of Jesus" that he would deny Him, and then Peter goes out and "wept bitterly". This was a trench and I can imagine he thought he had lost. I believe Peter would have left ministry if it hadn't been for the second prediction Jesus made that night at the Last Supper. Although, Jesus first predicted Peter's denial in John 13:36-38 we must remember his conversation doesn't end there but continues in chapter 14. Jesus reminded Peter of something we must remember in our darkest trench hours, *"Let not your heart be troubled; you believe in God, believe also in Me. In My Father's house are many mansions; if it were not so, I would have told you. I go to prepare a place for you. And if I go and prepare a place for you, I will come again and receive you to Myself; that where I am, there you may be also."* I would like to think visions of this hope and echoes of these words of Christ were what allowed Peter to get up and run down to the tomb early Resurrection morning and eventually up the temple steps preaching to 3,000 souls. He had been promised victory, so he ran back with Jesus into the trench of ministry.

Before I quit ministry, I must come face to face with my Savior who left everything to do trench ministry for me. Face to face with the one who has promised victory. And when I see Him, when I just catch a glimpse, my love for Him and His people moves me forward, yes right back into the trenches.

Reason #10 not to quit ministry:

We win in the trench!

Appendix

Tips for Creating Balance for the Minister

- Keep a tight schedule.
- Work Hard and Play Hard.
- Ensure there are streams that feed you.
- Remember who you are.
- Allowing God to minister to the minister.

10 Things Every Minister Should Be Doing

At least 2 hours of prayer each day.

1. Make intentional time for your Father, family, and friends.
2. Regularly read books in your field.
3. Visiting or calling team members.
4. Instituting processes and procedures that will outlast your tenure.
5. Coaching and training leaders.
6. Active entrenchment and engagement in the community.
7. Preaching doctrinal and relevant sermons/lessons.
8. Casting the ministry vision.
9. Practice what you preach.

A Weekly Guide for any Pastor

Sowing and Reaping P.O.W.E.R., by Pastor Terrance Taylor

Sunday – a day spent **SOWING** into your members or community. Meetings, visiting, outreach, preaching at a local church, whatever you do, spend this day pouring into people.

Monday – Prayer. Spend this entire day in prayer and Bible study. Listen for God's voice, reflect on yesterday's triumphs and challenges, bring these things before the Lord. Listen for a word to preach that is relevant to the issues you learned from the people on Sunday.

Tuesday – Organize. Gather your thoughts and strategize for the week. You should start gathering information for your sermon.

Wednesday – Work. Start putting your plans into action. Take calls, send emails, attend meetings, speak to council members, do Bible studies, beat the streets, etc. This is the day where you should come home exhausted. If you have time you can add more to your sermon.

Thursday – Evaluate. Take some time to review what you have done and take notes. You can spend this time talking with your mentor or reading books. By now you should be finishing up your sermon preparations.

Friday – Rest. Take this day off. Do something with your family, run some errands, play a game, watch a movie, you earned it. Sermon preparation should be over at the start of this day.

Saturday – This is the day you are **REAPING** from all the P.O.W.E.R. you have been sowing throughout the week. See where God has taken people and celebrate with them. Present your word to challenge and charge people for the next week. Lead the church in outreach or some relevant activity in the community.

About the Author

Pastor J. Nelson is an ordained minister of the gospel. He has been employed by the South Atlantic Conference of Seventh-day Adventist for the past ten years. He holds a BBA in Management, BA in Theology/Evangelism, and a MDiv. He is currently enrolled to complete his Doctorate in Ministry with the Urban Ministry Cohort. He is the Pastor of the Emmanuel SDA Church in Albany GA and Calvary SDA Church in Blakely, GA.

He is gifted in leadership, administration, financial management, teaching, and mission innovation. He is an up and coming activist, writer, and evangelist with a passion for social justice and community action. His life's purpose is spreading the Three Angel's messages through innovative methods for growth in God's Kingdom.

He is married to Kimberly Nelson, PH.d., an assistant professor of school counseling at Fort Valley State University. Father of two, Kaleah Jade and Jude King. Pastor Nelson enjoys traveling, sports, and spending time with his family.

Connect with Author

Joshua Nelson

@pjnelson25

pjnelson25@gmail.com

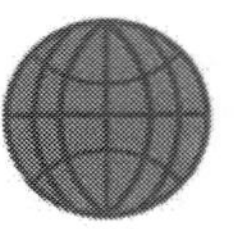

www.pastorjoshuanelson.com